Alexandru Prelipcean

Romanos' Renaissance

Studien zur Orientalischen Kirchengeschichte

herausgegeben von
Martin Tamcke

Band 61

Alexandru Prelipcean

Romanos' Renaissance

From the beginning to the present

Bibliography about Romanos the Melodist

LIT

Cover photo: Alexandru Prelipcean

Bibliographic information published by the Deutsche Nationalbibliothek
The Deutsche Nationalbibliothek lists this publication in the Deutsche
Nationalbibliografie; detailed bibliographic data are available on the Internet at
http://dnb.d-nb.de.

ISBN 978-3-643-91132-2 (pb)
ISBN 978-3-643-96132-7 (PDF)

A catalogue record for this book is available from the British Library.

© LIT VERLAG GmbH & Co. KG Wien,
Zweigniederlassung Zürich 2019
Klosbachstr. 107
CH-8032 Zürich
Tel. +41 (0) 44-251 75 05
E-Mail: zuerich@lit-verlag.ch   http://www.lit-verlag.ch
Distribution:
In the UK: Global Book Marketing, e-mail: mo@centralbooks.com
In North America: Independent Publishers Group, e-mail: orders@ipgbook.com
In Germany: LIT Verlag Fresnostr. 2, D-48159 Münster
Tel. +49 (0) 2 51-620 32 22, Fax +49 (0) 2 51-922 60 99, e-mail: vertrieb@lit-verlag.de
e-books are available at www.litwebshop.de

Content

Preface 7
Vowort 10
Note on this edition 13
Abbreviations 15
Bibliography about Romanos the Melodist 21
   1. Critical editions 21
   2. Modern translations 28
   3. Doctoral dissertations 34
   4. Works 36
   5. Dictionnaries&enciclopedias 39
   6. References from the Handbooks 44
   7. Studies&articles 50
   8. Notes 79

Preface

"Das Größte des christlichen Dichters" (*The magnificence of the Christian poet,* C.L.Ph. Meyer, 1906)

In the 19th and early 20th century, the leading encyclopaedias of the Protestant Church in Germany was the "Realencyklopädie für protestantische Theologie und Kirche" (*Real Encyclopaedia of Protestant Theological and Ecclesiastical Knowledge*). The 17th volume of the third edition of this encyclopaedia (Leipzig 1906) included an article that had not been in any of the previous editions: it was an article on Romanos. The length of the article alone was significant: seven pages were attributed to a man who had not even been mentioned up to this point. But the author of said article was also of note. It was the Lutheran Christian Ludwig Philipp Meyer (1854–1927), who was part of the leading body of the church in Hannover. He never held a professorship, merely served as the inspector of the Theological Seminary at Georg-August-University Göttingen in 1880–81 where he also spent a majority of his time as a student. Before he returned to the former Kingdom of Hannover in 1888 he had been priest in the German Lutheran congregation in Smyrna from 1881–1888. But he was mainly known for his function as editor of the standard work on Mount Athos: "Die Haupturkunden für die Geschichte der Athosklöster" (*The main documents on the history of the Athonite Monasteries,* published by J.C. Hinrichs, Leipzig 1894). He had done extensive research on Greek Orthodoxy and had written on the more recent history of the Athonite Monasteries, on the Prayer of the Heart, the Philokalia, as well as his most important publication "Die theologische Literatur der griechischen Kirche im 16. Jahrhundert" (*16th Century Theological Literature of the Greek Church,* Leipzig 1899). Meyer was keen to broaden the Protestants' understanding of orthodoxy. As a Lutheran from a background of rich church music traditions

(Johann Sebastian Bach himself had worked in the Kingdom of Hannover for several years) Meyer was passionate about the liturgical treasures of orthodoxy. This might explain why he opens his encyclopaedic entry with a phrase that already provides a suitable characterisation: "Romanos, größter Liederdichter der griechischen Kirche" (*Romanos, greatest hymnographer of the Greek Church*). Meyer answers all academic questions on Romanos that were relevant at his time, but for good reason, he adheres to the accounts of the Synaxarium. He takes a similar approach to any theological questions concerning Romanos. Meyer calls Romanos's poetry "dramatic" or "of delicate beauty" and for sections that might be deemed less convincing he explains: "Bei Romanos findet man auch das Größte des christlichen Dichters, er hat den Geist des Evangeliums in schöner Form zum Ausdruck gebracht, selbstverständlich auf dem Boden des zeitgeschichtlichen Christentums" (*Romanos also captures the magnificence of the Christian poet; he has given form to the essence of the Gospel, naturally, on the basis of contemporary Christianity*). This is, of course, a Protestant view on Romanos. Members of other denominations might have a different take on his works. But what is central here is that Meyer believes Romanos to have preserved the heart of Protestantism. This is not an attempt at making Romanos a Protestant; it is rather indicative of how highly regarded he was that complying with Meyer's standards inevitably elevated him to a father of theology and piety as well. Orthodoxy presumably denied such views or treated them with scepticism and thus the debate surrounding the message of the text intensified and still influences current practice.

Such a dispute among theologians over a text only highlights its significance. As Meyer says, Romanos is the greatest hymnographer of the Greek Church, or in other words: the Orthodox Church. When other denominations see in him a kindred spirit and honour him for what he was – a representative of the Orthodox Church – then they do not overstep the mark, but rather bow before a figure of significance who earned their appreciation. Meyer's conclusion is a conventional one: he opposes the usual disparaging criticism about the Byzantium era to the energetic report of Romanos, who, according to Meyer, defies static form.

Alexander Prelipcean, who taught in Iași, Romania, was the recipient of a scholarship at my institution in Göttingen where Meyer's tradition is carried on. Here he offers his bibliography on Romanos to the public in order to facilitate and promote further research. In this preface I not only want to commend Prelipcean's work, but based on our shared interest in the sources of the orthodox tradition, I also want to remind all churches with a regard for history to consider this a joint venture: the exploration of early ecclesiastical sources and their lasting impact. The list of publications speaks for itself. It is a long list which shows that Romanos continues to be studied, interpreted and that the impact of his texts never ceases. Should there be a second volume to this work, it would show: his influence persists! Prelipcean's bibliography is a reminder that Romanos still manages to stir emotions as well as revive the minds of researchers and through them the effect of Romanos's work continues.

Gratitude to Dr. Egbert Schlarb, Rauischholzhausen, for preparing the paper edition.

Martin Tamcke

Vowort

„Das Größte des christlichen Dichters" (Ph. Meyer, 1906)

Das bedeutendste Lexikon der protestantischen Kirche in Deutschland des 19. und frühen 20. Jahrhunderts war die „Realencyklopädie für protestantische Theologie und Kirche", und in diesem Lexikon erschien in dessen 3. Auflage im 17. Band (Leipzig 1906) ein Artikel, der in den beiden Auflagen zuvor nicht vorhanden war: ein Artikel zu Romanos. Schon der Umfang dieses Lexikonartikels war atemberaubend: 7 Seiten widmete das Lexikon einem Mann, der bis dahin nicht einmal erwähnt worden war. Und noch etwas ist dabei bemerkenswert: Der Verfasser dieses Artikels war der Lutheraner Christian Ludwig Philipp Meyer (1854–1927), der der Kirchenleitung in Hannover angehörte, aber nie eine Professur innehatte, sondern lediglich 1880/81 einmal kurz Inspektor des Theologischen Stiftes an der Georg-August-Universität in Göttingen gewesen war, an der er auch einen gewichtigen Teil seiner Studienzeit verbracht hatte. Bevor er 1888 ins ehemalige Königreich Hannover zurückkehrte, war er von 1881–1888 Pfarrer der deutschen lutherischen Gemeinde in Smyrna gewesen. Was ihn aber noch deutlicher auszeichnete: Er war der Herausgeber eines der wichtigsten Standardwerke zum Berg Athos, „Die Haupturkunden für die Geschichte der Athosklöster" (Verlag J. C. Hinrichs, Leipzig 1894), und hatte gründlich zur griechischen Orthodoxie recherchiert und Arbeiten zur neueren Geschichte und dem seinerzeit gegenwärtigen Zustand der Athosklöster, zum Herzensgebet, der Philokalie und sein wichtiges Buch „Die theologische Literatur der griechischen Kirche im 16. Jahrhundert" (Leipzig 1899) veröffentlicht. Meyer lag daran, die Kenntnisse zur Orthodoxie im protestantischen Raum zu vertiefen. Als Lutheraner selbst aus einer kirchenmusikalisch reichen Tradition kommend (selbst

Johann Sebastian Bach war ebenfalls einige Jahre im ehemaligen Königreich Hannover tätig gewesen), war er dem musikalischen und liturgischen Schatz der Orthodoxie aufgeschlossen. Und darum beginnt er seinen Lexikonartikel gleich mit einem Paukenschlag, indem schon im Eintrag zur Person diese von ihm einschlägig charakterisiert wird: „Romanos, größter Liederdichter der griechischen Kirche." Meyer stellt sich allen in seiner Zeit aufgeworfenen wissenschaftlichen Fragen zu Romanos, bleibt aber mit guten Gründen bei den Angaben des Synaxariums. Ähnlich stellt er sich zu damaligen theologischen Anfragen zu Romanos. Meyer nennt Romanos Dichtung „dramatisch" oder „von zarter Schönheit", und allen Beobachtungen zu weniger ihm überzeugend erscheinenden Partien erklärt er ganz grundsätzlich: „Bei Romanos findet man auch das Größte des christlichen Dichters, er hat den Geist des Evangeliums in schöner Form zum Ausdruck gebracht, selbstverständlich auf dem Boden des zeitgeschichtlichen Christentums." Das ist natürlich eine protestantische Sicht des Romanos. Angehörige anderer Konfessionen mögen ihre Sicht des Romanos anders ausdrücken. Zentral bleibt hier aber, dass das, was das Herz des Protestantismus ausmacht, von Meyer bei Romanos gewahrt sieht. Das ist nicht der Versuch, Romanos zu einem Protestanten zu machen, sondern der Versuch, ihn so wertzuschätzen anhand der eigenen Maßstäbe, dass er wie selbstverständlich zu einem Vater auch protestantischer Theologie und Frömmigkeit werden konnte. Orthodoxe Sichtweisen dürfen diese Sicht bestreiten oder mit Skepsis betrachten und damit eben das Ringen um die Aussage des Textes historisch ebenso wie für die Praxis in der Gegenwart intensivieren.

Solch ein Wettkampf der Theologen um einen Text erwiese nur dessen Attraktivität bis heute. Romanos ist eben der größte Liederdichter der griechischen Kirche, wie Meyer sagte, oder besser: der orthodoxen Kirche. Wenn andere Konfessionen in ihm einen Verwandten entdecken und seine Größe ehren als das, was er ist – ein Repräsentant der orthodoxen Kirchen –, dann werden sie gerade nicht übergriffig, sondern verneigen sich vor einer Größe, die auch sie überzeugt. Typisch ist Meyers Schluss. Der nur zu oft anzutreffenden abschätzigen Kritik an der Zeit der Byzantiner stellt er das vitale und seines Erachtens gerade nicht in Formeln erstarrte Zeugnis des Romanos entgegen.

Alexandru Prelipcean, der im rumänischen Iași lehrt, war 2017/18 Stipendiat in Göttingen an meinem Institut, das auch die Tradition Meyers fortführt. Was er hier der Öffentlichkeit als ein Hilfsmittel übergibt, ist seine Bibliographie zu Romanos, die weitere Forschungen erleichtern oder sogar erst motivieren könnte. Und dieses Vorwort möchte nicht nur die Arbeit Prelipceans empfehlen, sondern auch mit dem Hinweis auf unser gemeinsames Interesse an den Quellen orthodoxer Tradition darauf verweisen, dass alle Kirchen, die nicht einfach geschichtsvergessen sind, hier ein gemeinsames Werk vollziehen: die Erschließung von frühen kirchlichen Quellen und ihrer Wirkung bis heute. Die Liste der Publikationen allein schon bezeugt: Die Arbeit des Erschließens, Fortführens, Interpretierens und Nutzens dieser Texte ist lang und belegt so bereits aus sich heraus jenen bis heute anhaltenden Strom der Wirkung der Texte des Romanos.

Möchte in ein oder zwei Jahrzehnten ein Ergänzungsband notwendig werden, der zeigt: Die Wirkung bleibt! Prelipceans Werk macht uns allen wieder bewusst, wie Romanos bis heute nicht nur Gemüter, sondern auch die Geister der Forscher erregt hat und damit durch sie fortwirkt.

Ein Dank an Dr. Egbert Schlarb, Rauischholzhausen, für die zügige und effiziente Erstellung der Druckvorlage.

Martin Tamcke

Note on this edition

This work, which brings into light the bibliography, dedicated to Saint Romanos the Melodist, considered from the very beginning of the research by the author in question as 'the greatest of the poets of the Greek Church and of Christianity ... Pindar of the ecclesiastical poets'[1], does not claim its exhaustivity. This work intends to be primarily a useful tool for those who will focus their attention on the life, work and theology of the great Christian hymnographer from the time of Emperor Justinian.

The name of 'Romanos Renaissance' found in the title of this work is taken from the extremely captivating introduction of the volume of Sarah Gador-White, dedicated to *Theology and Poetry in Early Byzantium*[2]. We believe that all scholarly contributions, covering a period of two centuries, do nothing but revive the importance of Theological hymns, written by the 'humble Romanos' (τοῦ ταπεινοῦ Ῥωμανοῦ).

We have also proposed a fascinating excursion into the history of the critical editions, the contemporary translations of the Romanos writings, the Romanos' studies and articles, and the reviews of the existing monographs or translations. In some situations, the bibliographic references to Romanos the Melodist indicate certain kontakions, transposed on a linear notation[3]. For this reason, they have not been integrated into this bibliography dedicated to the Byzantine hymnographer.

---

[1] See: Νικ.Β. ΤΩΜΑΔΑΚΗΣ, 'Ῥωμανός. Ὁ Μελωδός', in *ΘΗΕ*, 10ος τόμος: Παπάς-Σατομπρίαν, Athens, 1960, 914; Π.Π.Κ., 'Ῥωμανός ὁ Μελωδός', in *Νεώτερον ἐγκυκλοπαιδικόν Λεξικόν. Μεθοδική καὶ συστηματικὴ συμπύνωσις καὶ ἐκλαΐκευσις ὅλων τῶν ἀνθρωπίνων γνώσεων*, vol. ιθ' [19], Athens, 1945, 599.

[2] See: Sarah GADOR-WHITE, *Theology and Poetry in Early Byzantium: The kontakia of Romanos the Melodist*, Cambridge University Press, Cambridge, 2017, ix.

[3] See, for example: [ANONYMUS], 'Kontakion from the Akathistos for the Dormition of the Mother of God', *JMP*, 1989, 8, 62-63; 'Kontakion on the nativity of Christ', *JMP*, 1991, 1, 78; 'Kontakion on the nativity of Christ, tone 3', *JMP*, 1991, 2, 77 etc.

Of course, I was not able to 'collect' here all the bibliographic materials dedicated to Romanos, although I initially proposed this. The difficulty came from the lack of knowledge of materials from many Oriental environments, which leaned less to Romanos research. However, I have recorded the most valuable studies from multiple spaces, and in terms of possible omissions or inaccuracies in this thematic bibliography I assume completely.

I want to thanks here to Professor Martin Tamcke from the Faculty of Theology in Göttingen, for his willingness to encourage me in this scientific approach and for the introduction of my study in the collection *Studien zur Orientalischen Kirchengeschichte*, as well as for the *Brot für die Welt*-Foundation from Berlin for the documentary scholarship offered in Göttingen.

Abbreviations

ABAW.PPH	*Abhandlungen der philos.-philol. und histor. Klasse der Bayer. Akademie der Wissenschaften*, München
ACl	*Acta Classica*, Kaapstad
Aevum	*Aevum. Rassegna di Scienze Storiche Linguistiche e Filologiche*, Milano
AFTOUB	*Anuarul Facultății de Teologie Ortodoxă a Universității din București*, București
AIVS	*Atti dell' Imperiale Istituto Veneto di Scienze, Lettere ed Arti*, Venezia
AMAT	*Atti e Memorie dell' Accademia Toscana la Colombaria*, Firenze
AnBoll	*Analecta Bollandiana*, Bruxelles
AnCl	*L'antiquité classique*, Bruxelles
At.	*Athenaeum, Studi periodici di lettratura e storia dell' antichità*, Pavia
Athēna	*Ἀθηνᾶ, Σύγγραμμα περιοδικόν τῆς ἐν Ἀθῆναις ἐπιστημονικῆς ἑταιρείας*, Athens
AuA	*Antike und Abendland*, Hamburg
Aug.	*Augustinianum*, Roma
BAGB	*Bulletin de l'Association Guillaume Budé*, Paris
BASPap	*Bulletin of the American Society of Papyrologists*, New Haven/Conn.
BBGG	*Bollettino della Badia Greca Grottaferrata*, Grottaferrata
BBKL	*Biographisch-bibliographisches Kirchenlexikon*, Hamm
Bess.	*Bessarione: rivista di studi orientali*, Roma
BGrL	*Bibliothek der Griechischen Literatur*, Stuttgart
BiRe	*Bible Review*, Washington
BMGS	*Byzantine and Modern Greek Studies*, London
BNGJ	*Byzantinisch-Neugriechische Jahrbücher*, Athens
BOR	*Biserica Ortodoxă Română*, București
BSS	*Bibliotheca Sanctorum*, Roma
ByS(P)	*Byzantine Studies: Études Byzantines*, Pittsburgh
Byz	*Byzantion, Revue internationale des études byzantines*, Bruxelles

Byz(T)	*Byzantina*, Thessalonika
ByZ	*Byzantinische Zeitschrift*, Leipzig
CbiPa	*Cahiers de Biblia Patristica*, Strasbourg
CKL	*Calwer Kirchenlexikon*, Stuttgart
ClR	*The Classical Review*, Oxford
ClW	*The Classical World*, New York
CM	*Classica et Medievalia*, København
CP	*Classical Philology*, Chicago
CSCO	*Corpus Scriptorum Christianorum Orientalium*, Roma
CtePa	*Collana di testi patristici*, Roma
DACL	*Dictionnaire d'archeologie chrétienne et de liturgique*, Paris
DECA	*Dictionnaire encyclopedique du christianisme ancient*, Paris
DMA	*Dictionary of the Middle Ages*, New York
DOP	*Dumbarton Oaks Papers*, Cambridge/Mass.
DPAC	*Dizionare patristico e di antichità cristiane*, Casale Monferrato
DSp	*Dictionnaire de spiritualité ascetique et mystique. Doctrine et histoire*, Paris
DThC	*Dictionnaire de théologie catholique*, Paris
EBrit	*Encyclopedia Britannica*, Chicago
EC	*Enciclopedia Cattolica*, Vatican
EcOra	*Ecclesia orans. Zur Einführung in den Geist der Liturgie*, Freiburg
EEBS	*Ἐπετηρὶς Ἑταιρείας Βυζαντινῶν Σπουδῶν*, Athens
EEThS	*Ἐπιστημονικὴ Ἐπετηρίδα Θεολογικῆς Σχολῆς Πανεπιστημίου Θεσσαλονίκης*, Thessalonika
Ekkl(A)	*Ἐκκλησία*, Athens
EkklAl	*Ἐκκλησιαστικὴ Ἀλήθεια*, Constantinople
EkklPh	*Ἐκκλησιαστικός Φάρος*, Alexandria
EncIt	*Enciclopedia italiana di scienze, lettere et arti*, Roma
EOr	*Échos d'Orient*, Bucureşti
EphMar	*Ephemerides Mariologicae*, Madrid
GBis	*Glasul Bisericii*, Bucureşti
Glotta	*Glotta. Zeitschrift für griechische und lateinische Sprache*, Göttingen
GOTR	*Greek Orthodox Theological Review*, Brookline/Mass.
GRBS	*Greek, Roman and Byzantine Studies*, Cambridge/Mass.

GrēgPal	*Γρηγόριος ὁ Παλαμᾶς*, Thessalonika
Hell.	*Ἑλληνικά, Φιλολογικόν, ἱστορικὸν καὶ λαογραφικόν περιοδικὸν σύγγραμμα*, Athens
Hermes	*Hermes. Zeitschrift für klassische Philologie*, Wiesbaden
HSCP	*Harvard Studies in Classical Philology*, Cambridge/Mass.
ICMS	*Atti del Congresso Internazionale di Musica Sacra*
IKBS	*Atti del Congresso Internazionale di Studi Bizantini*
JHS	*The Journal of Hellenic Studies*, London
JLH	*Jahrbuch für Liturgik und Hymnologie*, Kassel
JMP	*Journal of the Moscow Patriarchate*, Moscow
JÖB	*Jahrbuch der Österreichischen Byzantinistik*, Wien
JS	*Journal des savants*, Paris
JThS	*The Journal of Theological Studies*, Oxford
Kl.	*Κληρονομία*, Thessalonika
LThK	*Lexikon für Theologie und Kirche*, Freiburg
Mar.	*Marianum. Ephemerides Mariologiae*, Roma
MGG	*Die Musik in Geschichte und Gegenwart*, Kassel
MitrArd	*Mitropolia Ardealului*, Sibiu
MitrBan	*Mitropolia Banatului*, Timişoara
Muséon	*Le Muséon. Revue d'études orientales*, Louvain
NIDCC	*The New International Dictionary of the Christian Church*, Exeter
NS	New Series
NTS	*New Testament Studies. An International journal publ. under the auspices of Studiorum Novi Testamentum Societas*, Cambridge
NT.S	*Supplements to Novum Testamentum*
NTT	*Norsk Teologisk Tidsskrift*, Oslo
ODByz	*The Oxford Dictionary of Byzantium*, Oxford
ODCC	*The Oxford dictionary of the Christian church*, London
OrChr	*Oriens Christianus*, Roma
Ort	*Ortodoxia*, Bucureşti
OrthFor	*Orthodoxes Forum*, St. Ottilien
OS	*Ostkirchliche Studien*, Würzburg
RBPH	*Revue belge de philologie et d'histoire*, Bruxelles
RdT	*Rassegna di teologia*, Roma

RE	*Realenzyklopädie für protestantische Theologie und Kirche*, Leipzig
REA	*Revue des études anciennes*, Bordeaux
REByz	*Revue des études byzantines*, Paris
REG	*Revue des Études Grecques*, Paris
ReO	*Roma e l'Oriente*, Grottaferrata
RESEE	*Revue des Études Sud-Est Européennes*, București
RGG	*Die Religion in Geschichte und Gegenwart*, Tübingen
RHE	*Revue d'Histoire Ecclésiastique*, Louvain
RMM	*Revue de métaphysique et de morale*, Paris
RöHM	*Römische Historische Mitteilungen*, Graz
RPh	*Revue de philologie, de littérature et d' histoire anciennes*, Paris
RQH	*Revue des Questions Historique*, Paris
RSBN	*Rivista di studi bizantini e neoellenici*, Roma
RSLR	*Rivista di storia e letteratura religiosa*, Firenze
RSR	*Recherches de science religieuse*, Paris
RT	*Revista Teologică*, Sibiu
SAWW.PH	*Sitzungsberichte der Akademie der Wissenschaften in Wien. Philosphisch-Historische Klasse*, Wien
SBAW.PH	*Sitzungsberichte der philos.-philol. und histor. Klasse der klg. Bayer. Akademie der Wissenschaften*, München
SBNE	*Studi bizantini e neoellenici*, Roma
SC	*Sources Chrétiennes*, Paris
SEAug	*Studia Ephemeridis Augustinianum*, Roma
SecCen	*The second century*, Abilene
Spec.	*Speculum, A Journal of Medieval Studies*, Cambridge
StPatr	*Studia Patristica*, Berlin-Leuven
StTeol	*Studii teologice*, București
SvTK	*Svensk Teologisk Kvartalskrift*, Lund
TEE	*Θρησκευτικὴ καὶ ἠθικὴ ἐγκυκλοπαιδεία*, Athens
TPAPA	*Transactions and Proceedings of the American Philological Assosiation*, New York
Tr.	*Traditio. Studies in ancient and medieval history, thought and religion*, New York
TRE	*Theologische Realenzyklopädie*, Berlin
TV	*Teologie și Viață*, Iași
VigChr	*Vigiliae Christianae*, Amsterdam

VS	*La Vie Spirituelle*, Paris
VV	*Vizantijskij Vremennik. Byzantina chronika*, St. Petersburg
Worship	*Worship. A review concerned with the problems of liturgical renewal*, Collegeville/Minn.
ZPE	*Zeitschrift für Papyrologie und Epigraphik*, Bonn
ZRGG	*Zeitschrift für Religions- und Geistesgeschichte*, Köln

Bibliography about Romanos the Melodist

1. Critical editions

CAMMELLI, Giuseppe, *Romano il Melode. Inni*, col. 'Testi christiani', 2, Libreria Editrice Fiorentina, Firenze 1930;

> Reviews: [ANONYMUS], '*Testi cristiani con versione italiana a fronte. vol. I, Terapia dei morbi pagani, Vol. II, Inni, vol. III, De magistro; De vera religione, vol. IV, La mistagogea es altriscritti* by G. Manacorda; Teodoreto; Nicola Festa; Romano il Melode; Giuseppe Cammelli; S. Agostino; P. Domenico Rassi; S. Massimo Confessore; Rafaele Cantarella', *RMM*, vol. 39 (1932), 2, 15;
> CESSI, Camillo, 'G. Cammelli, *Romano il Melode*, Firenze, Edizione «Testi Cristiani», 1931, pp. 410', *Aevum*, vol. 5 (1931), 1, 91-94;
> DAWKINS, R.M., '*Testi Cristiani con versione italiana a fonte. Introduzione e commento. II. Romano il Melode: Inni* by Giuseppe Cammelli ...', *ClR*, vol. 46 (1932), 1, 41-42;
> GUILLAND, R., '*Romano il Melode. Inni, a cura di Giuseppe Cammelli*. Edizioni «Testi Cristiani» (Firenze, 1930), 409p ...', *REG*, vol. 45 (1932), 212, 348-349;
> KOCH, H., 'Cammelli, G., ed., Romano il melode. Inni (TCr 2), Florence, 1930, 407pp.', *ZKG*, 51 (1932), 568;
> M[AA]S, P., 'Romano il Melode. Inni. A cura di Giuseppe Cammelli', *ByZ*, vol. 31 (1931), 1, 430;
> PUECH, A., '*Testi cristiani* con versione italiana a fronte *introduzione commento, diretti da* G. Manacorda. – Romano il Melode, *Inni a cura di* G. Cammelli, 407 p., Firenze 1930 ...', *RPh*, 6 (1932), 192-194.

CARPENTER, Marjorie, 'Romanos and the Mystery Play of the East', in ROBINSON, Rodney Potter (ed.), *The University of Missouri Studies. A Quarterly of Research contents Philological Studies in honor or Walter Miller*, vol. 11 (1936), 3, 21-51;

GROSDIDIER DE MATONS, José, *Romanos le Mélode. Hymnes*, vol. I-V, *SC*, 99, 110, 114, 128, 283, Cerf, Paris 1964-1981;

> Reviews: [ANONYMUS], 'José Grosdidier de Matons – *Romanos Le Mélode. Hymnes*, Tome V. *Nouveau Testament* (XLVI-L) *et hymnes de*

circonstance (LI-LVI) (*SC* 283) – Les Éditions du Cerf, Paris, 1981, 556 p.', *REByz*, vol. 40 (1982), 281;
AMAND DE MENDIETA, Emmanuel, 'José Grosdidier de Matons – *Romanos Le Mélode. Hymnes*, Préface de Paul Lemerle. Introduction, texte critique, traduction et notes. Tome I. Ancien Testament (I-VIII). Paris, Les Éditions du Cerf, 1964, 430 pp. (Sources chrétiennes, 99)', *AnCl*, vol. 34 (1965), 1, 271-274;
-, 'José Grosdidier de Matons, *Romanos Le Mélode. Hymnes*. Introduction, texte critique, traduction et notes. Tome II. Nouveau Testament (IX-XX). Paris, Éditions du Cerf, 1965. 382 pp. (Sources Chrétiennes. 110)', *AnCl*, vol. 34 (1965), 2, 623-625;
-, 'José Grosdidier de Matons, *Romanos Le Mélode. Hymnes. Tome III. Nouveau Testament* (XXI-XXXI). Introduction, texte critique, traduction et notes. Paris, Éditions du Cerf, 1965. 368pp. (Sources Chrétiennes. 114)', *AnCl*, vol. 35 (1966), 1, 306-307;
-, 'José Grosdidier de Matons, *Romanos Le Mélode. Hymnes*. Introduction, texte critique, traduction et notes. *Tome IV*. Nouveau Testament (XXXII-XLV). Paris, Éditions du Cerf, 1967. 604 pp. (Sources Chrétiennes. 128)', *AnCl*, vol. 36 (1967), 2, 694-696;
BRANIŞTE, Ene, 'Romanos Le Melode, *Hymnes* (ediţie nouă), Paris, 1965', *Ort*, 18 (1966), 3, 448-459;
DALMAIS, I.H., 'José Grosdidier de Matons – Romanos Le Mélode. Hymnes, coll. «Sources chrétiennes», 99, 110, 114, Paris, Le Cerf', *Revue de l'histoire des religions*, vol. 169 (1966), 2, 214-215;
-, 'Romanos le Mélode. Hymnes, vol. V, introduction, texte critique, traduction et notes par J. Grosdidier de Matons, t. V, Nouveau Testament (XLVI-L) et Hymnes de circonstance (LI-LVI)', *Revue de l'histoire des religions*, vol. 200 (1983), 2, 228-229;
DARROUZÈS, Jean, 'Romanos le Mélode, *Hymnes*. Tome IV: *Nouveau Testament* (XXXII-LV). Introduction, texte critique, traduction et notes par Jean Grosdidier de Matons (SC, 128). Paris, Éditions du Cerf, 1967; 604p.', *REByz*, vol. 27 (1969), 278-279;
DES PLACES, Édouard, 'Romanos le Mélode, *Hymnes*. Préface de Paul Lemerle. Introduction, texte critique, traduction et notes par José Grosdidier de Matons. T. I. Ancien Testament (I-VIII). Tome II. Nouveau Testament (IX-XII) (Sources Chrétiennes, 99 et 110). Paris. Éditions du Cerf, 1964 et 1965. 429 et 381 pp.', *REG*, vol. 78 (1965), 369, 471-472;
-, 'Romanos le Mélode, *Hymnes*. Introduction, texte critique, traduction et notes par José Grosdidier de Matons. Tome III. *Nouveau Testament* (XXI-XXXI). (Sources Chrétiennes, 114). Paris, Éditions du Cerf, 1965, 368 pages', *REG*, vol. 79 (1966), 374, 568;

-, 'Romanos le Mélode, *Hymnes*. Introduction, texte critique, traduction et notes par José Grosdidier de Matons. Tome IV. *Nouveau Testament* (XXXII-XLV). (Sources Chrétiennes, 128). Paris, Éditions du Cerf, 1967, 603 pages', *REG*, vol. 81 (1968), 384-385, 315-316;

DORIVAL, Gilles, 'Romano le Melode, *Hymnes*, tome V, Introduction, texte critique, traduction et notes par José Grosdidier de Matons (Sources Chrétiennes, n° 238), Paris, Ed. du Cerf, 1981, 543 pages', *REA*, vol. 84 (1982), 1-4, 178-179;

GRYSON, R., 'Grosdidier de Matons (José). *Romanos le Mélode. Hymnes.* Tome V. *Nouveau Testament (XLVI-L) et Hymnes de circonstance (LI-LVI)*. Introduction, texte critique, traduction et notes. Paris, Éditions du Cerf, 1981; 1 vol., 544 p. (Sources Chrétiennes, 283)', *RBPH*, vol. 61 (1983), 1, 217;

LEROY-MOLINGHEN, Alice, 'José Grosdidier de Matons, *Romanos le Mélode, Hymnes.* Vol. V. Introduction, texte critique, traduction et notes. Paris. Les Éditions du Cerf, 1981, 556 pp. (Sources Chrétiennes. N° 283)', *AnCl*, vol. 52 (1983), 413;

LONGNON, Jean, '*Romanos le Mélode. Hymnes.* Introduction, texte critique, traduction et notes par José Grosdidier de Matons. Tome I: Ancient Testament (I-VIII), tomes II et III: Nouveau Testament (IX-XX et XXI-XXXI), Paris, Éditions du Cerf, 3 vol. in 16 de 429, 381 et 367p., 1964-1965 (*Sources chrétiennes*, n°s 99, 110, 114)', *JS*, vol. 1 (1966), 1, 61-64;

MOTTE, Laurent, 'Romanos le Mélode. *Hymnes V.* Éd. et trad. par J. Grosdidier de Matons, Collection Sources Chrétiennes, Éd. Cerf, Paris, 1981, 543p.', *REG*, vol. 95 (1982), 450, 223-224;

MUNITIZ, J., 'Romanos le Mélode. *Hymnes*. Introduction, texte critique, traduction et notes par José Grosdidier de Matons. Tome V: Nouveau Testament (XLVI-L) et hymnes de circonstance (LI-LVI) (Sources Chrétiennes, 283). Paris, Éditions du Cerf, 1981; Pp. 556', *VigChr*, vol. 36 (1982), 4, 406-409;

TOPPING, Eva C., 'José Grosdidier de Matons, *Romanos le Mélode, Hymnes*. Paris: Les Éditions du Cerf, 1964-67. 4 vols. (Sources Chrétiennes, Nos. 99, 110, 114, 128)', *GOTR*, vol. 14 (1969), 2, 226-227;

VAN GRONINGEN, B.A., 'Romanos le Mélode. *Hymnes*. Introduction, texte critique, traduction et notes par José Grosdidier de Matons. Tome I: Ancient Testament, I-VIII; Tome II: Nouveau Testament, IX-XX; Tome III: Nouveau Testament, XXI-XXXI; Tome IV: Nouveau Testament, XXXII-XLV (Sources Chrétiennes, 99, 110, 114, 128). Paris, Les Éditions du Cerf, 1964; 1965; 1967. Pp. 440; 382; 368; 604.', *VigChr*, vol. 22 (1968), 2, 157-158;

WELLESZ, Egon, '*Romanos le Mélode, Hymnes*. Préface de Paul Lemerle. Introduction, Texte Critique, Traduction, et Notes par José Grosdidier de Matons, 4 volumes. Pp. 429+381+369+603. (Sources Chrétiennes, nos. 99, 110, 114, 128.) Paris: Les Éditions du Cerf, 1964, 1965, 1965, 1967.', *JThS*, NS, vol. 20 (1969), 2, 657-666.

KRUMBACHER, Karl, 'Studien zu Romanos', *SBAW.PH*, vol. 2 (1898), 1, 69-268 (republished: Verlag der K.B. Akademie der Wissenschaften, München 1899);

> Reviews: MONTMASSON, E., 'K. Krumbacher. *Miscellen zu Romanos*, Munich, Académie des sciences, 1907, 136 pages in-4° avec une planche', *EOr*, vol. 12 (1909), 76, 189;
> PETIT, L., 'K. Krumbacher, *Studien zu Romanos*, Sitzungsber. der philos.-philol. und histor. Classe K. bayer. Akad. d. Wiss., München, 1898, Bd. II. Heft I, p. 69-268', *EOr*, vol. 2 (1899), 6, 316-317;
> R., T., 'Krumbacher (Karl). *Studien zu Romanos*. Extrat des Sitzungsberichte de l'Acad. de Munich, 1898, II, p. 69-268', *REG*, vol. 12 (1899), 47, 338-339.

-, 'Umarbeitungen bei Romanos. Mit einem Anhang über das Zeitalter des Romanos', *SBAW.PH*, vol. 2 (1899), 1-156 (republished: Verlag der k. Akademie, München 1900);

> Reviews: PETIT, L., 'K. Krumbacher, *Umarbeitungen bei Romanos, mit einem Anhang über das Zeitalter des Romanos*. Sitzungster. der philos.-phil. und der histor. Classe der k. Bayer-Akad. d. Wiss. 1899, Bd. II, Heft I, 156 pages', *EOr*, vol. 3 (1900), 5, 318-319;
> R., T., 'Krumbacher (Karl). *Umarbeitungen bei Romanos*. Munich, Franz, 1898, 156 p. (Extrait des *Sitzungsberichte* de l'Ac. de Bavière, 1899)', *REG*, vol. 13 (1900), 53-54, 418-419.

-, 'Romanos und Kyriakos', *SBAW.PH*, 1901, 693-763 (republished: Verlag der K.B. Akademie der Wissenschaften, München 1902);

> Reviews: LE BEAU, A., ' K. Krumbacher. *Romanos und Kyriakos*. Tirage à part des Sitzungsberichte de l'Acad. de Munich, 1901, p. 693-766', *REG*, vol. 15 (1902), 67, 474.
> VAILHE, S., 'K. Krumbacher: *Romanos und Kyriakos*. Extrait des *Sitzungsberichten der philos.-philol. und der histor. Classe der Kgl.*

> *Bayer. Akademie der Wissenschaften*, 1901, p. 693-766', *EOr*, vol. 5 (1902), 6, 405.

-, 'Die Akrostichis in der griechischen Kirchenpoesie', *SBAW.PH*, 1903, 4, 551-692 (republished: Verlag der K.B. Akademie der Wissenschaften, München 1904);

> Reviews: [ANONYMUS], 'Karl Krumbacher, *Die Akrostichis in der griechischen Kirchenpoesie* (extrait des Sitzungsberichte de l'Acad. de Bavière, 1903, p. 551-591)', *REG*, vol. 17 (1904), 78, 487; PETIT, L., 'K. Krumbacher, *Die Akrostichis in der griechischen Kirchenpoesie*, Munich, imprimerie de l'Académie, 1904. Extrait des *Sitzungsberichte der philos.-philol. und der histor. Klasse*, 1903, fasc. IV, p. 551-691', *EOr*, vol. 7 (1904), 49, 380.

-, 'Miscellen zu Romanos', *ABAW.PPH*, vol. 24, 3, Verlag der K.B. Akademie der Wissenschaften, München 1907, 1-138;

> Review: MONTMASSON, E., 'K. Krumbacher, *Miscellen zu Romanos*. Munich, Académie des sciences, 1907, 136 pages', *EOr*, vol. 12 (1909), 76, 189.

-, 'Der heilige Georg in der griechischen Überlieferung', *ABAW.PPH*, vol. 25, 3, Verlag der Königlich Bayerischen Akademie der Wissenschaften, München 1911, 1-332;

ΛΙΒΑΔΑΡΑ, Νικολάου Α., *Τὸ πρόβλημα τῆς γνησιότητας τῶν ἁγιολογικῶν ὕμνων τοῦ Ῥωμανοῦ*, Ἐναίσιμος ἐπὶ διδακτορίᾳ διατριβὴ ὑποβληθεῖσα εἰς τὴν Φιλοσοφικὴν Σχολὴν τοῦ Ἐθνικοῦ καὶ Καποδιστριακοῦ Πανεπιστημίου Ἀθηνῶν, Τυπογραφεῖον Μηνᾶ Μυρτίδη, Ἀθῆναι 1959, 131-158;

> Review: G., R., 'Livadaras (N. A.), Τὰ προβλήματα τῆς γνησιότητος τῶν ἁγιολογικῶν ὕμνων τοῦ Ῥωμανοῦ. Athènes, 1959, 170 p.', *REG*, vol. 74 (1961), 349-350, 344.

MAAS, Paul, 'Das Weihnachtslied des Romanos', *ByZ*, vol. 24 (1923-1924), 1, 1-13;

-, Trypanis, C.A., *Sancti Romani Melodi Cantica*, vol. I: *Cantica genuina*, At the Clarendon Press, Oxford, 1963; vol. II: *Cantica dubia*, Walter de Gruyter, Berlin 1970;

> *Reviews*: Amand de Mendieta, Emmanuel, 'Paul Maas (†) et C.A. Trypanis, *Sancti Romani Melodi Cantica. Cantica dubia*. Berlin, Walter de Gruyter&Co, 1970, xx-223 pp.', *AnCl*, vol. 40 (1971), 1, 299-301;
> Grosdidier de Matons, J., '*Sancti* Romani *Melodi Cantica. Cantica genuina*. Edited by Paul Maas and C.A. Trypanis. Oxford, Clarendon Press, 1963. In-8°, xxvi-547 p.', *REG*, vol. 76 (1963), 361, 505-508;
> Hunger, H., 'Sancti Romani Melodi Cantica. Cantica genuina. Ed. by Paul Maas and C.A. Trypanis. Oxford, Clarendon press 1963. Xxxviii, 547 S.', *ByZ*, vol. 57 (1964), 2, 437-443;
> Livadaras, N.A., 'A propos d'une nouvelle édition de Romanos le Mélode', *Athēna*, vol. 67 (1964), 20-32;
> McCail, Ronald C., 'Romanos the Melodist. Cantica: cantica dubia. Ed. P. Maas and C.A. Trypanis. Berlin: W. de Gruyter. Pp. xx+223', *JHS*, vol. 91 (1971), 159-160;
> Musurillo, Herbert, 'Paul Maas and C.A. Trypanis (edd.). *Sancti Romani Melodi Cantica: Cantica Genuina*. Oxford: Clarendon Press; New York: Oxford University Press, 1963. Pp. xxxvii, 547', *ClW*, vol. 57 (1964), 6, 279.

Mioni, Elpidio, *Romano il Melode. Saggio critico e dieci inni inediti*, G.B. Paravia, Torino 1937;

> *Review*: Sbordone, F., 'E. Mioni, *Romano il Melode*. Saggio critico e dieci inni inediti, G.B. Paravia, Torino, 1937', *At.*, NS, vol. 17 (1939), 102.

-, 'Romano il Melode. Due inni sul S. Natale', *BBGG*, NS, vol. 12 (1958), 3-17;

Παπαδοπουλοσ-Κεραμευσ, Ἀ., 'Ἀθωνικὰ κονδακαρίων ἀντίγραφα', *ByZ*, vol. 6 (1897), 2, 383-386;

Παπαγιαννησ, Γρηγόριος, 'Ῥωμανοῦ τοῦ Μελῳδοῦ κοντάκιον «εἰς τὴν Σαμαρείτιδα». Νέα κριτικὴ ἔκδοση μὲ παρατηρήσεις', *Byz(T)*, vol. 33 (2014), 11-59;

PARANIKAS, M./CHRIST, W., *Anthologia graeca carminum christianorum*, In Aedibus B.G. Teubneri, Lipsiae 1871, 90-91, 131-140;
PITRA, Joannes Baptista, *Hymnographie de l'Église grecque*, Imprimerie de la Civiltà Cattolica, Roma 1867, i-x;
-, *Analecta Sacra Specilegio Solesmensi parata*, tom. I, A. Jouby et Roger, Bibliopolis, Paris 1876, 1-241;
-, *Sanctus Romanus veterum melodorum princeps*, Cantica sacra ex codicibus mss. Monasterii S. Johannis in insula Patmo primum in lucem ed. J. B. Pitra, anno Jubilaei Pontifici, Roma 1888, 1-55;
ΤΩΜΑΔΑΚΗ, Νικολάου Β., *Ρωμανοῦ τοῦ Μελῳδοῦ ὕμνοι*, ἐκδιδόμενοι ἐκ πατμιακῶν κωδίκων, τόμος I-IV, Τυπογραφεῖον Μηνᾶ Μυρτίδη, Αθῆναι 1952-1959;

> Reviews: ΚΟΜΙΝΗ, Ἀθανασίου, 'Ἡ ἔκδοσις τοῦ Α' τόμου τῶν ὕμνων Ρωμανοῦ τοῦ Μελῳδοῦ', *Athēna*, vol. 57 (1953), 377-389;
> ASTRUC, Charles, 'Markos Naoumidis et Panayotis Nikolopoulos, Τὰ Κοντακάρια τῆς Πάτμου (Κώδικες 212 καὶ 213 ΙΑ' αἰῶνος). – Athènes, M. Myrtidis, 1954, 395 p.', *BAGB*, 2 (1955), 108-109;
> -, 'Nikolaos A. Livadaras, Κοντακάρια τοῦ Σινᾶ (Ρωμανοῦ τοῦ Μελῳδοῦ Ὕμνοι, Τόμος τρίτος, Μέρος Α',), Athènes, M. Myrtidis, 1957, 461 pp.', *BAGB*, 3 (1957), 91-92;
> ΒΑΣΙΛΙΚΟΠΟΥΛΟΥ, Ἀγνή, 'Ρωμανικὰ Σύμμεικτα Α' – Παρατηρήσεις καὶ ἐπανορθώσεις εἰς τὸν κς' Ὕμνον', *Athēna*, vol. 59 (1955), 78-80;
> GUILLAND, R., '*Tomadakis (Nicolas B.)*. Ρωμανοῦ τοῦ Μελῴδου Ὕμνοι ἐκδιδόμενοι ἐκ Πατμιακῶν κωδίκων. Τόμος πρῶτος. Athènes, 1952, κδ' et 335p.', *REG*, vol. 66 (1953), 311, 530-531;
> -, 'Ρωμανοῦ τοῦ Μελῴδου Ὕμνοι ἐκδιδόμενοι ἐκ Πατμιακῶν κωδίκων μετὰ προλεγομένων ὑπὸ Νικολάου Β. Τωμαδάκη. Τόμος δεύτερος. Athènes, 1954, xx-τζδ'+392 p. (= 806 p.)', *REG*, vol. 69 (1956), 324, 263;
> -, 'Ρωμανοῦ τοῦ Μελῳδοῦ Ὕμνοι. Ἔκδοσις κριτική. Τόμος τρίτος. Μέρος Β': ὕμνοι ΚΘ'-ΛΣ' μετ' εἰσαγωγῶν, σχολίων, μεταφράσεως καὶ πινάκων. Ἀφιέρωμα εἰς Ν.Β. Τωμαδάκην. Athènes, 1957, 400p.', *REG*, vol. 72 (1959), 339, p. 469;
> -, 'Ρωμανοῦ τοῦ Μελῴδου. Ὕμνοι. Ἔκδοσις κριτική. Τόμος τέταρτος. Μέρος Α': Ὕμνοι ΛΖ'-Μ'. Athènes, 1959, 183 p.', *REG*, vol. 74 (1961), 349, 343;
> JOANNOU, P., '"Ὕμνοι εἰς τοὺς ἁγίους Δημήτριον καὶ Νικόλαον ἐκ χειρογράφων ἐκδιδόμενοι. Athen, Druckerei M. Myrtides (Sonder-

abdruck aus dessleben Verfassers Ῥωμανοῦ τοῦ Μελῳδοῦ Ὕμνοι, Τόμος Β'). 83 S., 1 Bl.', *ByZ*, vol. 48 (1955), 1, 142-154;
ΚΟΜΙΝΗΣ, Δ. Ἀθανάσιος, 'Ἡ ἐκδόσις τοῦ α' τόμου τῶν ὕμνων Ῥωμανοῦ τοῦ Μελῳδοῦ', *Athēna*, vol. 57 (1953), 377-389;
ΛΙΒΑΔΑΡΑΣ, Νικόλαος Α., 'Ῥωμανικὰ Σύμμεικτα Γ' – Διορθώσεις καὶ προσθῆκαι εἰς τὸν Β' τόμον', *Athēna*, vol. 59 (1955), 83-85;
Ρ., Μ., 'Ῥωμανοῦ τοῦ Μελῳδοῦ· *Ὕμνοι, ἔκδοσις κριτικὴ*. Τομ. ΙΙΙ, μέρ. β'. Ἀθῆναι, 1957. 400 p.', *BBGG*, NS, vol. 12 (1958), 133-134;
SEVERIEN, Salaville, 'Tomadakis (N. B.), Ῥωμανοῦ τοῦ Μελῳδοῦ Ὕμνοι ἐκδιδόμενοι ἐκ Πατμιακῶν κωδίκων, t. I, Athènes, 1952, in-8°, κδ'-336 pages, fac-similé en frontispice', *REByz*, vol. 12 (1954), 250-252;
Τ., Ν.Β., 'Ῥωμανικὰ Σύμμεικτα Β' – Παρατηρήσεις καὶ ἐπανορθώσεις εἰς τὸν Α' τόμον τῶν ὕμνων', *Athēna*, vol. 59 (1955), 80-83.

TRYPANIS, C.A., *Fourteen Early Byzantine Cantica*, col. 'Wiener Byzantinistische Studien', 5, Wien 1968.

> Reviews: DARROUZÈS, Jean, 'C.A. Trypanis, *Fourteen early byzantine Cantica*, (Wiener byz. Studien. 5), Vienne, H. Böhlhaus, 1968; 171 p.', *REByz*, vol. 27 (1969), 279-280;
> G., R., 'Trypanis (C.A.). *Fourteen Early Byzantine Cantica* (Wiener Byzantinische Studien, Band V), Wien, H. Böhlaus Nachf., 1968, 171 p.', *REG*, vol. 82 (1969), 389-390, 272-273.

ΤΖΙΑΤΖΗ-ΠΑΠΑΓΙΑΝΝΗ, Μαρία, 'Το κοντάκιο του Ρωμανού του Μελωδού «Εἰς τὸν χωλὸν τὸν παρὰ τὴν πύλην τοῦ ἱεροῦ θεραπευθέντα ὑπὸ τῶν Ἀποστόλων» (αρ. 39 M.-Tr.): Φιλολογικές παρατηρήσεις και νέα κριτηκή έκδοση', *Byz(T)*, vol. 29 (2009), 63-109;
-, 'Das zweite Kontakion des Pseudo-Romanos auf den Heiligen Nikolas (= Maas-Trypanis 78)', *Byz(T)*, vol. 30 (2010), 25-54.

2. Modern translations

[ANONYMUS], 'Condacul Naşterii lui Iisus', in Petre VINTILESCU, *Despre poezia imnografică din cărţile de ritual şi cântare bisericească*, Renaşterea, Cluj-Napoca ²2005, 189-204;

AERTS, Willem J./HOKWERDA, Hero/SCHOONHOVEN, Henk, *Romanós de Melode. Vier Byzantijnse hymnen en de Akáthistoshymne*, Styx Publications, Groningen 1990;
ALVETEG, Kristina, 'Romanos Melodos: Ett ytterligare kontakion för Stora Fredagen till Herrens lidande och Guds föderskans klagan', in *Svenskt patristiskt bibliotek*, IV: Bibel och predikan, Sten HIDAL (ed.), Artos 2003, 183-201;
BALLING, Jakob, 'Menneskers Eneste Ven. Romanós' kontákion om Elias', col. 'Under Guds Ord', 344, Skive 1997;
BARKHUIZEN, J.H., 'Romanos the Melodist. Verse homily «On the newly baptised»', *Acta Patristica et Byzantina*, vol. 11 (2000), 1-21 (the English translation of the kontakion 'On the newly baptised', 2-9);
-, 'Romanos the Melodist: «On Adam and Eve and the Nativity»: Introduction with Annotated Translation', *Acta Patristica et Byzantina*, vol. 19 (2008), 1-22;
BARNEA, Ion M. et alii, 'Condacul Naşterii lui Hristos', traducere de studenţii teologi de la seminarul de Liturgică (în special Ion M. Barnea), in VINTILESCU, Petre, *Despre poezia imnografică din cărţile de ritual şi cântare bisericească*, Tipografia Cărţilor Bisericeşti, Bucureşti 1937, 290-306 [taking over of this translation by Alexăndrel BARNEA, 'Fecioara, astăzi', *Candela Moldovei*, 2 (1993), 11-12, 1;
-, 'Sfântul Roman Melodul, *Condacul Crăciunului*', *Candela Moldovei*, 2 (1993), 11-12, 3;
-, 'Condacul Crăciunului', *TV*, NS, 3 (1993), 11-12, 15-28];
BIGEL, Jean-Pierre/MARSAUX, Jacky, *Romanos le mélode: l'année en hymnes*, col. 'Bibliothèque', 5, Migne, Paris 2014;
ΒΛΑΧΟΣ, Ε., *Ρωμανοῦ Μελωδοῦ: Ὕμνος Ἁγίων Ἀποστόλων*, Ἀθῆναι 1973;
BULTMANN, Gabriel Henning, *Romanus der Melode: Festgesänge auf Christgeburt, auf Theophanie, auf den Ostersonntag*, Thomas, Zürich 1960;
BUNTA, Silviu, 'Condacul Naşterii lui Hristos', *RT*, NS, 8 (1997), 4, 146-153;

CARPENTER, Marjorie, *Kontakia of Romanos, Byzantine Melodist*, I: *On the person of Christ*, II: *On Christian life*, University of Missouri Press, Columbia 1970-1973;
  Reviews: BANDY, Anastasius C., 'Marjorie Carpenter (tr.). Kontakia of Romanos. Byzantine Melodist. I: On the Person of Christ. Translated and annotated. Columbia, Mo.: University of Missouri Press, 1970. Pp. xlvi, 380; frontisp.', *ClW*, vol. 66 (1973), 5, 300;
  TRYPANIS, C.A., '«*Kontakia*» *of Romanos, Byzantine Melodist,* I: *On the Person of Christ*. Translated and Annotated by Marjorie Carpenter. Columbia: University of Missouri Press, 1970, Pp. xliv+380 +frontispiece', *CP*, vol. 70 (1975), 2, 154.

ΔΑΛΛΑ, Γιάννη, *Ρωμανοῦ τοῦ Μελωδοῦ. Εἰς τὰ ἅγια νήπια*, Τό πρωτότυπο κείμενο σέ μετάφραση καὶ ἐπίμετρο τοῦ Γιάννη Δάλλα καὶ τριαντακτώ παράλληλα δημιουργήματα μέ μολύβι τοῦ Αγγ. Γερακάρη, Ἐκδόσεις Ἀπόστροφος, Κέρκυρα 1999;

DECARREAUX, Jean, 'Romain le Mélode: Thrène de la Vierge sur la Passion du Seigneur', *VS*, vol. 98 (1958), 243-258;

ENACHE, Laura, 'Imnul femeii păcătoase', *TV*, NS, 12 (2002), 9-12, 204-215;

-, 'Imnul fiului risipitor', *TV*, NS, 15 (2005), 7-12, 40-53;

FRĂCEA, Ilie, 'Imnul Învierii lui Lazăr', *MitrArd*, 20 (1975), 6-8, 502-507;

GHARIB, Georges, *Romano il Melode. Inni*, Edizioni Paoline, Figlie di San Paulo, Torino 1981;

GRIGORIU, Paraschiva, *Imnele pocăinței*, studiu introductiv de Andrew Louth, traducere și note de Parascheva Grigoriu, Trisaghion, Iași 2006;

GROSDIDIER DE MATONS, José, *Romanos le Mélode. Hymnes*, vol. I-V, *SC*, 99, 110, 114, 128, 283, Éditions du Cerf, Paris 1964-1981;

ΧΑΡΑΛΑΜΠΙΔΗΣ, Κυριάκος, *Ρωμανοῦ τοῦ Μελωδοῦ: τρεῖς ὕμνοι*, Ἐκδόσεις Ἄγρα, Ἀθῆνα 1997 (two of the three hymns were previously published under the title: *Ρωμανός ὁ Μελωδός. Εἰς τὴν Ἁγίαν Γέννησιν τοῦ Κυρίου ἡμῶν Ἰησοῦ Χριστοῦ*, Ὀρθόδοξο Πνευματικό Κέντρο Λεμεσοῦ, Λευκωσία 1988);

-, *Ρωμανός ὁ Μελωδός. Εἰς τὴν Ἀνάστασιν τοῦ Κυρίου*, Μετάφραση Κυριάκος Χαραλαμπίδης, Σημάτωρος, Λευκωσία 1988;

HUNGER, Herbert, *Reich der Neuen Mitte: der christliche Geist der byzantinischen Kultur*, Styria, Graz 1965, 217-221, 224-226;
KHAWAM, René R., *Romanos le Mélode. Le Christ Redempteur. Célébration liturgies*, introduction de I.-H. Dalmais, Beauchesne, Paris 1956;

> Reviews: GRUMEL, V., 'Romanos le Mélode, *Le Christ Rédempteur. Célébrations liturgiques*. Traduit du grec par Renè R. Kawam, Paris, Beauchesne, 1956, 183 pages', *REByz*, vol. 16 (1958), 255-256;
> GUILLAND, R., 'Khawam (René R.). *Romanos le Mélode. Le Christ rédempteur. Célébrations liturgiques*. Traduit du grec. Paris 1956, 181p. Avec une Préface de Irénée-Henri Dalmais', *REG*, vol. 70 (1957), 331, 564;
> V., S., '*Romanos le Mélode, Le Christ Rédempteur. Célébrations liturgiques*, Traduit du grec par René R. Karwan, Beauchesne, Paris, 1956, 183 p.', *StTeol*, 11 (1959), 7-8, 503.

KOCHLAMAZASHVILI, E., GAMBASHIDZE, A., 'Romanos Melodosis sašobao kontakionis żveli kartuli targmani', *Bizantinistika sakartveloši. Eżghvneba akademikos Simon Kauxčišvili*, Tblisi 2007, 356-360;
KODER, Johannes, *Mit der Seele Augen sah er deines Lichtes Zeichen Herr. Hymnen des orthodoxen Kirchenjahres von Romanos dem Meloden*, Verlag der Österreichischen Akademie der Wissenschaften, Wien 1996;
-, *Romanos Melodos. Die Hymnen*, vol. 1-2, BGrL, 62-64, Anton Hiersemann, Stuttgart 2005-2006;

> Review: CONTICELLO, Vassa, 'Johannes Koder (trad.), *Romanos Melodos. Die Hymnen*. Übersetzt und erläutert von Johannes Koder, I-II (Bibliothek der griechischen Literatur 62 und 64). – Anton Hiersemann, Stuttgart 2005 et 2006; relié. x-433 p. (I), vi p.-p. 435-478 (II)', *REByz*, vol. 66 (2008), 278-279.

ΚΟΥΣΤΕΝΗΣ, Ἀνανίας, *Ῥωμανοῦ Μελῳδοῦ. Ὕμνοι*, τόμος 1-2, Χ. Μπούρας, Ἀθήνα 1997 (republished in the volume: *Ῥωμανοῦ Μελῳδοῦ. Ὕμνοι*, Ἐκδόσεις Ἁρμός, Ἀθήνα 2003);

ΚΟΥΤΡΟΥΜΠΑ, Δημητρίου Εὐθ., *Ῥωμανοῦ τοῦ Μελωδοῦ ὕμνοι: κοντάκιον κατανυκτικόν*, Τῇ Τεράρτῃ τῆς β' ἑβδομάδος τῶν νηστειῶν (῞Υμνος μη'), Τυπογραφεῖον Μυρτίδης, Ἀθῆναι 1974;

KOZHOUSHNIY, Pr. Oleg, *Преподобний Роман Солодкоспівець і візантійська гімнографія III-VIII столітъ.*, Київська Духовна Акадумія, Видавничий Відділ Укрфїнської Православної Церкви, Kiev 2009;

LASH, Ephrem, *On the Life of Christ: Chanted Sermons by the Great Sixth-Century Poet and Singer St. Romanos*, Harper-Collins, San Francisco 1996 (^{2}2010, Yale University Press);

MAISANO, Riccardo, *Cantici di Romano il Melodo*, vol. 1-2, col. 'Classici greci – Autori della tarda antichità e della grecità bizantina', Unione Tipografico-Editrice Torinese, Torino 2002;

> *Reviews*: CONCA, Fabrizio, 'Riccardo Maisano (ed.), *Cantici di Romano il Melodo*, vol. I-II, Torino, UTET 2002, 646+663 p.', *ByZ*, vol. 96 (2003), 2, 743-747;
>
> NERI, Marino, 'In margine a una recente edizione di Romane il Melode', *At.*, vol. 93 (2005), 2, 647-651;
>
> PERNOT, Laurent, 'Riccardo Maisano, *Cantici di Romano il Melodo*. Torino: Unione Tipografico-Editrice Torinese (Classici Greci: Autori della tarda antichità e dell' età bizantina), 2002. 2 volumes, 646+668 pages', *Rhetorica: A Journal of the History of Rhetoric*, vol. 23 (2005), 2, 205-207.

MANGOGNA, Viviana/TROMBI, Ugo, *Romano il Melode, Kontakia*, vol. 1-2, *CTePa*, 197-198, Città Nuova, Roma 2007;

ΠΑΣΧΟΣ, Παντελής Β., *Ῥωμανὸς ὁ Μελωδὸς καὶ Ἅγιος Παντελεήμων*, Εἰσαγωγικά-κείμενον τοῦ ὕμνου-ἀνάλυσις, Τυπογραφεῖον Ἀποστολική Διακονία, Ἀθῆναι 1979;

PREDA, Sabin, 'Luna lui iulie în douăzeci de zile. Condac la pomenirea Sfântului Prooroc Ilie', *StTeol.NS*, 4 (2008), 3, 143-165;

PRELIPCEAN, Alexandru, 'Condacul *La nunta cea din Cana*', in *Studia Theologica Doctoralia*, vol. 3, Viorel SAVA et alii (eds.), Doxologia, Iaşi, 2011, 397-405;

-, 'Sfântul Roman Melodul, [Condac] la *Naşterea Maicii Domnului*', *Almanah bisericesc 2013: Studii teologice şi aspecte pastoral-*

misionare, Episcopia Sloboziei și Călărașilor, Slobozia 2013, 169-174 [republished in: *Orizonturi teologice*, NS, 13 (2013), 2, 91-98];
-, 'Condac *La toți sfinții*', *Ort*, NS, 8 (2016), 4, 138-143;
-, 'Condac *La neofiți*', in Alexandru PRELIPCEAN, *'Cuvinte, dă-mi cuvinte'. De la viața 'smeritului Roman' la teologia poetică a Melodului bizantin*, Astra Museum, Sibiu 2017, 259-271;
-,/IORGA, Alexandru, *Sfântul Roman Melodul, Imne teologice*, col. 'Patristica. Traduceri', 3, Doxologia, Iași 2012;

> *Review*: PEREGRINUS, 'Imne teologice. Sfântul Roman Melodul. Editori (traducere din greacă veche, studiu introductiv și note): Alexandru Prelipcean și Alexandru Iorga, Editura Doxologia, Iași, 2012', *Convorbiri literare* 147, 6 (iun. 2013), 179.

-, *Sfântul Roman Melodul, Imnele Sfintei Scripturi*, col. 'Patristica. Traduceri', 4, Doxologia, Iași 2012;
RODRIGUEZ, Marcelo Merino, *Romano el Cantor: Himnos*, vol. 1-2, col. 'Biblioteca de Patrística', Ciudat Nueva, Madrid, 2012-2013;
ROGOBETE, Cristina Costena, 'Imnul I al Epifaniei', *AFTOUB*, vol. 2 (2001-2002), 439-499;
-, 'Imnul II al Epifaniei', *AFTOUB*, vol. 2 (2001-2002), 499-506;
-,/PREDA, Sabin, *Sfântul Roman Melodul, Imne*, Bizantină, București 2007;

> *Review*: PRELIPCEAN, Alexandru, 'Sf. Roman Melodul, *Imne*, traducere, studiu introductiv și note Cristina Rogobete și Sabin Preda, București, 2007, 336 p.', *Ort*, NS, 1 (2009), 3, 203-207.

SCHORK, R.J., *Sacred Song from the Byzantine Pulpit: Romanos the Melodist*, University Press of Florida, Gainesville 1995;

> *Review*: THEOKRITOFF, Elizabeth, 'R.J. Schork, *Sacred Song from the Byzantine Pulpit: Romanos the Melodist* (Gainesville: University of Florida Press, 1995), XVI+230 pp.', *International Journal of the Classical Tradition*, vol. 5 (1999), 4, 612-614.

SCOGNAMIGLIO, P. Rosario, *Inni di Romano il Melode*, col. 'Studi e Testi', 1, Centro Studi di S. Nicolai, Bari 1985;

ΣΙΝΟΠΟΥΛΟΣ, Π.Α., *Ῥωμανοῦ τοῦ Μελῳδοῦ. Κοντάκια α'*, ὅπως τὰ εἶχε μεταφράσει ὁ Π.Α. Σινόπουλος, που τὰ παρουσιάζει μὲ μία προθεωρία, Ἐκδόσεις Ἀποστολικῆς Διακονίας, Ἀθῆναι 1974;
ΣΩΦΡΟΝΙΟΣ, Λ., 'Ῥωμανού του Μελωδού: Ψαλμὸς εἰς τὸ ἅγιον Πάσχα', *GrēgPal*, 1 (1917), 31-39.

3. Doctoral dissertations

ARENTZEN, Thomas, *Virginity Recast: Romanos and the Mother of God*, Faculty of Theology, Lund University, Lund 2014;

ERIKSEN, Uffe Holmsgaard, *Drama in the Kontakia of Romanos the Melodist: A Narratological Analysis of Four Kontakia*, PhD dissertation, Graduate School of Arts, Aarhus University, Aarhus 2013;

> Review: BODIN, Helena, 'Uffe Holmsgaard Eriksen, *Drama in the Kontakia of Romanos the Melodist: A Narratological Analysis of Four Kontakia*, Aarhus: Graduate School of Arts, Aarhus University, 2013', *Kyrkohistorisk årsskrift*, 2014, 135-140.

GADOR-WHYTE, Sarah Elizabeth, *Rhetoric and Ideas in the Kontakia of Romanos the Melodist*, Submitted in total fulfilment of the requirements of the degree of Doctor of Philosophy, Center for Classics and Archaeology, The University of Melbourne, Melbourne 2011;

GEERTRUI, Van den Eynde, *Romanos Melodos: de eerste Kersthymne*, University of Leuven, Leuven 1992;

GROSDIDIER DE MATONS, José, *Romanos le Mélode et les origines de l'hymnographie byzantine*, Lille 1974 (published as a book: *Romanos le Mélode et les origines de la poésie religieuse à Byzance*, Préface de Paul Lemerle, Collection dirigée par Charles Kannengiesser, Beauchesne, Paris 1977);

> Reviews: DARROUZES, Jean, 'José Grosdidier de Matons, *Romanos le Mélode et les origines de la poésie religieuse à Byzance*. Préface de Paul

Lemerle (collection Beauchesne Religions). – Editions Beauchesne, Pa-Paris, 1977, xix-338 p.', *REByz*, vol. 37 (1979), 275-276;
LEROY-MOLINGHEN, Alice, 'Grosdidier de Matons (José). *Romanos le Mélode et les origines de la poésie religieuse à Byzance.* Paris, Beauchesne, 1977', *RBPH*, vol. 58 (1980), 3, 667-668;
M., H., 'J. Grosdidier de Matons, *Romanos le Mélode et les origines de la poésie religieuse à Byzance*, Préface de Paul Lemerle, Beauchesne, Paris, 1977, 338 p.', *RESEE*, vol. 16 (1978), 3, 595-596;
SANSTERRE, Jean-Marie, 'José Grosdidier de Matons, *Romanos le Mélode et les origines de la poésie religieuse à Byzance*, Préface de Paul Lemerle, Paris, Beauchesne, 1977, xix+338 p. (Beauchesne Religions)', *AnCl*, vol. 48 (1979), 1, 325-327;
TONNET, H., 'Grosdidier de Matons (J.), *Romanos le Mélode et les origines de la poésie religieuse à Byzance*, Beauchesne, Paris, 1977, xix+338 p.', *REG*, vol. 93 (1980), 442, 612-613.

IORGA, Alexandru, *Η πορεία προς τη σωτηρία. Τα ανθρωπολογικά στοιχεία των κοντακίων του Ρωμανού του Μελωδού*, Εκδόσεις Μπαρμπουνάκη, Θεσσαλονίκη 2017;
ΚΟΡΑΚΙΔΟΥ, Ἀλεξάνδρου Σ., *Ἡ περὶ τοῦ λόγου θεολογία τῶν κονδακὶων Ρωμανοῦ τοῦ Μελῳδου*, διατριβὴ ἐπί διδακτορίᾳ, ὑποβληθεῖσα εἰς τὴν Θεολογικὴν Σχολὴν τοῦ Πανεπιστημίου Θεσσαλονίκης, Ἐκδόσεις Ἰωνία, Ἀθῆναι 1973;
ΚΟΥΡΕΜΠΕΛΕ, Ἰωάννη Γ., *Ἡ χριστολογία τοῦ Ρωμανοῦ τοῦ Μελωδοῦ καὶ ἡ σωτηριολογικὴ σημασία τῆς*, Διατριβή ἐπί διδακτορίᾳ, ὑποβληθεῖσα στὸ τμῆμα Θεολογίας τῆς Θεολογικῆς Σχολῆς τοῦ Ἀριστοτελείου Πανεπιστημίου, Θεσσαλονίκης 1998;

> *Romanian translation*: KOUREMBELES, Ioannis G., *Hristologia Sfântului Roman Melodul şi importanţa ei soteriologică*, translated by Alexandru Prelipcean, Doxologia, Iaşi 2018;
> *Review*: PRELIPCEAN, Alexandru, 'Ἰωάννης Γ. Κουρεμπελές, *Ἡ Χριστολογία τοῦ Ρωμανοῦ τοῦ Μελωδοῦ καὶ ἡ σωτηριολογικὴ σημασία της*, διατριβή ἐπί διδακτορίᾳ, Θεσσαλονίκη, 1998, 310σσ. [Ioannnis G. Kourembeles, *Hristologia lui Roman Melodul şi importanţa ei soteriologică*, teză de doctorat, Tesalonic, 1998, 310 pp., în manuscris]', *Ort*, NS, 7 (2016), 3, 273-279.

ΛΙΒΑΔΑΡΑ, Νικολάου Α., *Τὸ πρόβλημα τῆς γνησιότητας τῶν ἁγιολογικῶν ὕμνων τοῦ Ῥωμανοῦ*, Ἐναίσιμος ἐπὶ διδακτορίᾳ διατριβὴ ὑποβληθεῖσα εἰς τὴν Φιλοσοφικήν Σχολήν τοῦ Ἐθνικοῦ καὶ Καποδιστριακοῦ Πανεπιστημίου Ἀθηνῶν, Τυπογραφεῖον Μηνᾶ Μυρτίδη, Ἀθῆναι 1959;

MULARD, Christelle, *La pensée symbolique de Romanos le Mélode*, CBiPa, 16, Brepols Publishers, Turnhout 2016;

MURESANU, Teodora Ilinca, *Teologia şi melodica imnelor Sfântului Roman Melodul*, Universitatea 'Babeş-Bolyai', Cluj-Napoca 2016;

PLISHKA, Andrew, *Christology and the Marian Kontakia of Saint Romanos the Melodist*, A Thesis submitted to the Faculty of the Graduate School of Loyola University of Chicago in Partial Fullfillment of the Requirements for the Degree of Master of Arts, Loyola University of Chicago, Chicago 1983;

REICHMUTH, Roland Joseph, *Typology of the Genuine Kontakia of Romanos the Melodist*, University of Minnesota, Minneapolis 1975;

SCHORK, R.J., *The Sources of the Christological Hymns of Romanos the Melodist*, University of Oxford, Oxford 1957;

TSIRONIS, Niki J., *The Lament of the Virgin Mary from Romanos the Melode to George of Nicomedia: An aspect of the development of the Marian Cult*, Departament of Byzantine and Modern Greek Studies, King's College London, London 1998;

ZANNINI, Paolo, *I 'Kontakia' di Romano il Melode sull' annunciazione: contenuti e fonti*, Pontificium Istitutum Orientale, Roma 1997.

4. Works

ARENTZEN, Thomas, *The Virgin in Song: Mary and the Poetry of Romanos the Melodist*, University of Pennsylvania Press, Philadelphia 2017;

> Review: MELLAS, Andrew, 'The Virgin in Song: Mary and the Poetry of Romanos the Melodist, By Thomas Arentzen, Pennsylvania: University

of Pennsylvania Press, 2017', *Church History: Studies in Christianity and Culture*, 87 (2018), 4, 1192-1194.

ΔΡΙΤΣΑΣ, Δημήτριος Λ., *Ὁ ἔρρυθμος πατερικός λόγος εἰς τὴν ἱστορικὴν ἐξέλεξιν. Ἡ προϊστορία τοῦ κοντακίου*, Ἱερά Μητρόπολη Ἠλείας, Ἀθῆναι 1986;

DUFFNER, Maria H., *Romanos der Melode: ... denn für uns wurde geboren ein kleines Kind, der urewige Gott*, Gedanken zu einem alten griechischen Weihnachtshymnus, Fluhegg, Gersau 2001;

ΕΥΣΤΡΑΤΙΑΔΗΣ, Σωφρόνιος, *Ῥωμανός ὁ Μελωδός καὶ ἡ Ἀκάθιστος*, Σ. Παντελή&Ν. Ξενοφωντίδου, Θεσσαλονίκη 1917;

> *Review*: ÉMEREAU, A., 'Mgr Sophrone Eustratiadès, Ρωμανὸς ὁ Μελωδὸς καὶ ὁ Ἀκάθιστος (= *Romain le Mélode et l'Acathiste*). Salonique, librairie Pantélis et Xénophontidès, 1917, 64 pages', *EOr*, vol. 19 (1920), 118, 247-248.

GADOR-WHITE, Sarah, *Theology and Poetry in Early Byzantium: The kontakia of Romanos the Melodist*, Cambridge University Press, Cambridge 2017;

ΚΟΡΑΚΙΔΗ, Ἀλεξάνδρου Σ., *Τὸ πρόβλημα τῆς καταγωγῆς τοῦ Ῥωμανοῦ τοῦ Μελωδοῦ, Συστηματική ἔρευνα τοῦ θέματος ἐκ τῶν πηγῶν καὶ ἐκθέσις τῶν ἀντισημιτικῶν στοιχείων τῶν κοντακίων*, Ἀθῆναι 1971;

-, *Ῥωμανοῦ τοῦ Μελῳδοῦ ὕμνος καὶ λόγος (δύο μελέτες)*, col. 'Φιλοσοφική καὶ θεολογική βιβλιοθήκη', 18, Ἐκδόσεις Π. Πουρναρᾶ, Θεσσαλονίκη 1990;

-, *Τὰ περὶ τοῦ Ῥωμανοῦ τοῦ Μελῳδοῦ μελετήματα*, ἔκδοσις συμπληρωμένη, Ἐκδόσεις Π. Πουρναρᾶ, Θεσσαλονίκη 2002;

ΚΟΥΡΕΜΠΕΛΕΣ, Ι.Γ., *Ῥωμανοῦ Μελῳδοῦ θεολογικὴ δόξα – σύγχρονη ἱστορικοδογματικὴ ἄποψη καὶ ποιητικὴ θεολογία*, Ἐκδόσεις Π. Πουρναρᾶ, Θεσσαλονίκη 2006 (²2010);

> *Romanian translation*: KOUREMBELES, Ioannis G., *Viziunea teologică a Sfântului Roman Melodul. Opinia istorico-dogmatică contemporană și teologia poetică*, translated by Alexandru Prelipcean, col. 'Patristica. Studii', 4, Doxologia, Iași 2013.

Reviews: COMAN, Claudiu-Ioan, 'Ioannis G. Kourembeles, *Viziunea teologică a Sfântului Roman Melodul. Opinia istorico-dogmatică contemporană şi teologia poetică*, colecţia «Patristica. Studii», vol. 4, Editura Doxologia, Iaşi, 2013, 217 p.', *TV*, NS, 23 (2013), 9-12, 194-203 [republished in: *Ort*, NS, 6 (2014), 2, 261-268];
PRELIPCEAN, Alexandru, 'Ι.Γ. Κουρεμπελές, *Ρωμανού Μελωδού Θεολογική Δόξα. Σύγχρονη ιστορικοδογματική άποψη καί ποιητική θεολογία*, Εκδ. Π. Πουρναρά, Θεσσαλονίκη, 2006, 331 σσ. [I.G. Kourempeles, *Faima teologică a lui Roman Melodul. Opinia istoricodogmatică contemporană şi teologia poetică*, Editura P. Pournara, Tesalonic, 2006, 331pp.]', *TV*, SN, 20 (2010), 9-12, 202-207.

ΛΕΝΤΑΚΗΣ, Ανδρέας, *Ρωμανός ο Μελωδός, Κώστας Βάρναλης και στρατευμένη τέχνη*, Εκδόσεις Δωρικός, Αθήνα 1991;

MITSAKIS, K., *The Language of Romanos the Melodist*, C.H. Beck, München 1967;

Review: DARROUZÈS, Jean, 'K. Mitsakis, *The language of Romanos the melodist*. (Byzant. Archiv., 11.), C.H. Beck, München,1968; (20)+217 p.', *REByz*, vol. 27 (1969), 310.

PETERSEN, William L., *The Diatessaron and Ephrem Syrus as Sources of Romanos the Melodist*, CSCO, 475 (Subsidia 74), Louvain 1985;

Reviews: BUNDI, David, 'William L. Petersen, *The Diatessaron and Ephrem Syrus as Sources of Romanos the Melodist (CSCO 475, Subsidia 74)* – Louvain 1986. xxxiv-216 p.', *SecCen*, vol. 8 (1991), 3, 179-181;
MAHÉ, Jean-Pierre, 'William L. Petersen, *The Diatessaron and Ephrem Syrus as Sources of Romanos the Melodist (CSCO 475, Subsidia 74)* – Louvain 1986. xxxiv-216 p.', *REByz*, vol. 44 (1986), 317-318;
MURRAY, Robert P.R., 'William L. Petersen, *The Diatessaron and Ephrem Syrus as Sources of Romanos the Melodist (CSCO 475, Subsidia 74)* – Louvain 1986. xxxiv-216 p.', *JThS*, vol. 40 (1990), 1, 258-260.

PETRESCU, I.D., *Condacul Naşterii Domnului – Ἡ Παρθένος σήμερον. Studiu de muzicologie comparată*, Bucureşti 1940;

Review: GOUILLARD, J., 'Petrescu (I.D.), *Condacul Naşterii Domnului* Ἡ παρθένος σήμερον [Le Kontakion de Noël]. *Studiu de muzicologie comparată*. Bucurest, 1940, *ByS(P)*, vol. 1 (1943), 1, 291-292.

PRELIPCEAN, Alexandru, *'Cuvinte, dă-mi cuvinte'. De la viaţa 'smeritului Roman' la teologia poetică a Melodului bizantin*, Astra Museum, Sibiu 2017;

SENARD, Charles, *Le dialogues des 'Puissances Infernales' dans l'oeuvre de Romanos le Mélode*, Directeur de recherche: Bernand Flusin, DEA de Grec, Université de Paris IV-Sorbonne, Paris 2004 (in manuscript);

ΣΙΝΟΠΟΥΛΟΣ, Π.Α., *Βίος καὶ πολιτεία τοῦ ἐν ἁγίοις πατρός ἡμῶν Ῥωμανοῦ τοῦ Μελωδοῦ: ἡ ἁγιότητα του καὶ ἡ ποιητική μεγαλωσύνη του*, Ἐκδόσεις Ὀρθόδοξος Τῦπος, Ἀθῆναι 1982;

ΤΣΙΑΜΗ, Μήτσου Ν., *Ρωμανός ο Μελωδός*, Εκδόσεις Παπαδήμας, Αθήνα 2006;

WEHOFER, Thomas M., *Untersuchungen zum Lied des Romanos auf die Wiederkunft des Herrn*, SAWW.PH, vol. 154, 5, Wien 1907.

> Review: SALAVILLE, S., 'T.-M. Wehofer, *Untersuchungen zum Lied des Romanos auf die Wiederkunft des Herrn ...*', *EOr*, vol. 13 (1910), 80, 53-54.

ΞΥΔΗ, Θεοδώρου, *Ῥωμανός ὁ Μελωδός στὰ Χριστούγεννα καὶ Θεοφανεία*, Ἐκδόσεις Ἀκτίνες, Ἀθῆναι 1949 (republished in: *Βυζαντινή υμνογραφία*, Ἐκδόσεις «Νικόδημος», 1978, 25-51).

5. Dictionnaries&enciclopedias

[ANONYMUS], 'Romanos', in *CKL*, Kirchlich-theologisches Handwörterbuch, Friedrich REPPLER (ed.), vol. 2, L-Z, Calwer, Stuttgart 1941, 760;

[ANONYMUS], 'Ῥωμανὸς, - 1: ὁ Μελωδός', in *Γενική Πανκόσμιος Ἐγκυκλοπαιδία. Μετά πλήρους Λεξικού τῆς ἑλληνικῆς γλώσσης*, Ἐπὶ τη βάσει τῆς γενικῆς ἐγκυκλοπαιδικῆς ὕλης τοῦ «Grand Larousse Encyclopédique» προσαρμοσθείσης ὑπὸ τῆς ἐπιστημονικῆς ἑταιρείας τῶν ἑλληνικῶν γραμμάτων «Πάπυρος», vol. 11 [32], Πάπυρος, Ἀθήνα 1963, 655;

[ANONYMUS], 'Ρωμανὸς ὁ Μελωδὸς', in *Παγκόσμιον Λεξικόν τῶν ἔργων: ἐπιστημῆς-τέχνης-φιλοσοφίας*, vol. 5, Διεθνής Ἐκδοτικός Ὀργανισμός Spiritus Mundi, Ἀθῆναι 1966, 2099-2100;
[ANONYMUS], 'Romanos (d. 556)', in *NIDCC*, J.D. DOUGLAS (ed.), The Paternoster Press, Exeter 1974, 858;
[ANONYMUS], 'Romano il Melode', in *Lessico Universale Italiano di lingua Lettere Arti Scienze e Tecnica*, Umberto BOSCO (ed.), vol. 19: Ricl-Sanf, Istituto della Enciclopedia italiana, Roma 1978, 344;
[ANONYMUS], 'Ρωμανός ο Μελωδός', in *Γενική Ἐγκυκλοπαιδεία Σύγχρονων γνώσεων. Ὑδρια-Cambridge-Ἥλιος*, vol. 10: Περθ-Σαντάτ, Ἐκδόσεις Τέσσερα Ἔψιλον, Ἀθήνα 1992, 3466;
[ANONYMUS], 'Romanos, St.', in *ODCC*, F.L. CROSS, Margaret LADZ (eds.), Oxford University Press, Londra-New York-Toronto ³1997, 1411;
[ANONYMUS], 'Romanus the Melodist, St.', in *The Books of Saints. A Comprehensive Biographical Dictionary*, Dom Basil Watkins, OSB on behalf of the Benedictine monks of St. Augustine's Abbey, Ramsgate, Bloomsbury T&T Clark, London, ⁸2016, 650;
AMANN, É., 'Romanos le Mélode', in *DThC*, A. VACANT et alii (eds.), vol. 13, deuxieme partie: Quadratus-Rosmini, Libraire Letouzey et Ané, Paris 1937, 2895-2898;
ARRANZ, M., 'Romanos le Mélode', in *DSp*, Marcel VILLER et alii (eds.), vol. 13: Raban Maur-Ryelandt, Beauchesne, Paris 1937, 898-908;
BALDWIN, B., 'Romanos the Melode', in *ODByz*, Alexander P. KAZHDAN et alii (eds.), Prepared at Dumbarton Oaks, vol. 3, Oxford University Press, New York-Oxford 1991, 1807-1808;
BREILMANN, B., 'Romanus der Sänger', in *Lexikon der antiken christlichen Literatur*, Siegmar Döpp und Wilhelm Geerlings (eds.), unter Mitarbeit von Peter Bruns, Georg Röwekamp, Matthias Skeb OSB, Freiburg-Basel-Wien ²1999, 535-536;
BUCHWALD, Wolfgang et alii (eds.), 'Romanos', in *Dictionnaire des Auteurs Grecs et Latins de l' Antiquite et du Moyen Age*, traduit et

mis à jour par Jean Denis Berger et Jacques Billen, Brepols 1991, 757-758;

CABROL, F., LECLERQ, H., 'Hymnes', in *DACL*, Fernard CABROL, Henri LECLERCQ (eds.), vol. 6, Deuxiéme partie, VI Librairie Letouzey et Ané 87, Paris 1925, 2881-2882;

CANTARELLA, Raffaele, 'Romano il Melòde', in *EC*, Pio PASCHINI (ed.), vol. 10: Pri-Sbi, Ente per L'enciclopedia Cattolica e per il Libro Cattolico, Città del Vaticano 1953, 1310-1311;

COOPER, J.C. (ed.), 'Romanus the Melodist, St', in *Cassell. Dictionary of Christianity*, Cassel, London and Washington 1997, 233;

CORSINI, Eugenio, 'Romano il Melode', in *Grande Dizionario Enciclopedico Utet*, Pietro FEDELE (ed.), Terza editione interamente riveduta e accresiuta, vol. 16, Unione Tipografico-Editrice Torinese, Torino 1971, 262-263;

CULERRIER, Pascal, 'Romanos le Mélode', in *Encyclopaedia Universalis*, Thesaurus-Index, Rapa-Zyriane, Paris 2002, 3981;

ENGBERG, Gudrun, LINGAS, Alexander, 'Romanos the Melodist', in *The New Grove: Dictionary of Music and Musicians*, Stanley SADIE (ed.), vol. 21: Recitatice to Russian Federation, Grove 2001, 595;

FRIZ, K., 'Romanos, der Melode', in *Evangelisches Kirchenlexicon*, Heinz BRUNOTTE, Otto WEBER (eds.), Kirchlich-theologische Handwörterbuch, P-Z, 2. unveränderte Auflage, Vandenhoeck& Ruprecht, Göttingen 1959, 669-670;

GRESCHAT, Martin, 'Romanos der Melode', in *Personenlexikon Religion und Theologie*, Vandenhoek&Ruprecht, Göttingen 1998, 404;

HANNICK, Christian, 'Romanos der Melode', in *MGG*, vol. 14: Personenteil Rich-Schön, Bärenreiter-Metzler, Kassel-Stuttgart 2005, 330-331;

HÖRANDNER, Wolfram, 'Romanos Melodos', in *LThK*, vol. 8: Pearson bis Samuel, Herder, Freiburg 1999, 1278-1279;

KODER, Johannes, 'Romanos Melodos', in *Marienlexikon*, Remigius BÄUMER, Leo SCHEFFCZYK (eds.), EOS, St. Ottilien 1993, 538;

-, 'Romanos der Melode', in Hans Dieter BETZ et alii (eds.), *RGG*, vol. 7: R-S, Mohr-Siebeck, Tübingen ⁴2004, 603;

KÖTTING, B., 'Romanos der Melode', in *LThK*, Josef HÖFER und Karl RAHNER (eds.), vol. 9: Rom bis Tetzel, Herder, Freiburg 1964, 16-17;

KRAFT, Heinrich, 'Romanus', in *Kirchenväter-Lexikon*, Kösel, München 1966, 446;

LAMPADARIDI, Anna, 'Romanos le Mélode (fin V^e-milieu VIe siècle)', in *La Bible dans les literatures du monde*, J à Z, Sylvie PARIZET (ed.), Cerf, Paris 2016, 1882-1884;

McHUGH, Michael P., 'Romanus Melodus (ca. 485-ca. 560)', in *Encyclopedia of Early Christianity*, Everett FERGUSON et alii (eds.), Gerland publishing, New York-London 1990, 796-797 (²1998, 996-997);

MERCATI, S.G., 'Romano il Melode', in *EncIt*, Giovanni GENTILE, Calogero TUMMINELLI (eds.), vol. 30, Publicata sotto l'alto patronato di S.M. il re d'Italia, Istituto Giovanni Treccani, Roma 1936, 59-60;

MEYER, Ph., 'Romanos', in *RE*, Johann Jakob HERZOG, Albert HAUCK (eds.), vol. 17: Riesen-Schutzheilige, Leipzig 1906, 124-131;

Π., Π.Κ., 'Ῥωμανός ὁ Μελωδός', in *Νεώτερον ἐγκυκλοπαιδικόν Λεξικόν. Μεθοδική καὶ συστηματικὴ συμπύνωσις καὶ ἐκλαΐκευσις ὅλων τῶν ἀνθρωπίνων γνώσεων*, vol. 19, Ἐκδόσεις τῆς Ἐγκυκλοπαιδικῆς Ἐπιθεωρήσεως «Ἥλιος», Ἀθῆναι 1945, 599-600;

ΠΑΝΤΕΛΑΚΗ, Ε.Γ., 'Ῥωμανός ὁ μελωδός', in *Μεγάλη Ἑλληνικὴ Ἐγκυκλοπαίδεια*, Παῦλος ΔΡΑΝΔΑΚΗΣ (ed.), vol. 21, Ἐκδοτικός Ὀργανισμός «Ὁ Φοῖνιξ», Ἀθήνα 1934, 307-308;

PELTOMAA, Leena Mari, 'Romanos the Melode', in *The Encyclopedia of Ancient history*, Roger S. BAGNALL et alii (eds.), MA: Wiley-Blackwell, Malden 2012, 5881;

PLESTED, Marcus, 'Romanos Melodos', in *A Dictionary of Jewish-Christian Relations*, Edward KESSEL and Neil WENBORN (eds.), Cambridge University Press, Cambridge 2005, 383;

ROSSER, John H., 'Romanos the Melode', in *Historical Dictionary of Byzantium*, Historical Dictionaries of Ancient Civilizations and Historical Eras, no. 4, The Scarecrow Press, Lanham/Maryland and London 2001, 345;

RUS, Remus, 'Roman Melodul', in *Dicţionarul enciclopedic de literatură creştină din primul mileniu*, Lidia, Bucureşti 2003, 743-744;

SA., K., 'R. Melodos, «der Melode»', in *Der Neue Pauly Enzyklopädie der Antike*, Hubert CANCIK und Helmuth SCHNEIDER (eds.), vol. 10: Pol-Sal, J.B. Metzler, Stuttgart-Weimar 1996, 1127-1128;

STIERNON, Daniele, 'Romano il Melode', in *BSS*, Filippo CARAFFA (ed.), Istituto Giovanni XXIII della Pontificia Università Lateranense, Città Nuova Editrice, Roma 1968, 319-323;

SURMANN, B., 'Romanus der Sänger', in *Lexikon der Antiken Christlichen Literatur*, Siegmar DÖPP und Wilhelm GEERLINGS (eds.), Herder, Freiburg im Breisgau ³1998, 612;

T.A., Ce., 'Romanos, Saint', in *EBrit*, vol. 19: Raynal to Sarraut, William Benton Publisher, Chicago-London-Toronto-Geneva 1964, 455;

TIMUŞ, Gherasim, 'Roman (Melodul)', in *Dicţionar aghiografic cuprinzând pe scurt vieţile Sfinţilor*, Tipografia Cărţilor bisericeşti, Bucureşti, 1898, 720 (²1998, Mănăstirea 'Portăriţa', Satu Mare 776);

TINNEFELD, Franz, 'Romanos der Melode', in *BBKL*, Friedrich E. BAUTZ, Traugott BAUTZ (eds.), vol. 8: Rembrandt bis Scharbel, Traugott Bautz, Herzberg 1994, 633-636;

ΤΩΜΑΔΑΚΗΣ, Νικ. Β., 'Ῥωμανός. Ὁ Μελῳδός', in *ΤΕΕ*, Ἀθανάσιος ΜΑΡΤΙΝΟΣ (ed.), vol. 10: Παπάς-Σατομπρίαν, Ἐκδόσεις Ἀθανάσιος Μαρτίνος, Ἀθήνα 1960, 914-921;

TRYPANIS, C.A., 'Romanos', in *RGG*, vol. 5: P-Se, J.C.B. Mohr (Paul Siebeck), Tübingen 1961, 1166;

VELIMIROVIĆ, Miloš, 'Romanos Melodos, St.', in *DMA*, Joseph R. STRAYER (ed.), vol. 10: Polemics-Scandinavia, Charles Scribner's Sons, New York 1988, 516-517;

WALSH, Michael, 'Romanus Melodus', in *Dictionary of Christian Biography*, Continuum, London-New York, 2001 1036;

ZINCONE, S., 'Romano il Melode', in *DPAC*, Angelo DI BERARDINO (ed.), vol. 2: GZ, Institutum Patristicum Augustinianum, Casa Editrice Marietti, Roma 1983, 3031-3032;

> *French translation*: ZINCONE, S., 'Romanos le Mélode', in *DECA*, Angelo DI BERARDINO (ed.), adaptation Française sous la direction du François Vial, vol. 2: J-Z, Cerf, Paris 1990, 2181-2182;
> *English translation*: ZINCONE, S., 'Romanus Melodus', in *Encyclopedia of the Early Church*, Angelo DI BERARDINO (ed.), Translated from the Italian by Adrian Walford, With a foreword and bibliographic amendments by W.H.C. Frend, vol. 2, James Clarke&Co., Cambridge 1992, 740.

-, LOUTH, Andrew, 'Romanus der Melode', in *TRE*, Horst BALZ et alii (eds.), vol. 29: Religionspsychologie-Samaritaner, Walter de Gruyter, Berlin-New York 1998, 396-400;

ZWAHR, Annette (ed.), 'Romanos', in *BI Universal Lexicon*, vol. 4: Moto/Seil, VEB Bibliographisches Institut, Leipzig 1990, 355.

6. References from the Handbooks

[ANONYMUS], 'Le même jour, mémoire de notre saint Père Romanos le Melode', in *Le Synaxaire. Vies des Saints de l'Eglise Orthodoxe*, Adaptation française par Macarie, moine de Simonos-Petras, tome premier: Septembre, Octobre, Novembre, Éditions To Perivoli tis Panaghias, Thesalonique, 1987, 211-212 [²2008, Indiktos, 320-321; Romanian translation: 'Tot în această zi, pomenirea Preacuviosului Părintelui nostru Roman Melodul', in *Sinaxarul Vieţile Sfinţilor*, Ierom. MACARIE de la Simonos Petras (ed.), translated by Rasofora Irina, Ioana Căpităneanu, Elena Soare, volumul II: luna Octombrie, Editura Sfântul Ioan Casian, Bucureşti 2013, 10-11];

[ANONYMUS], 'Luna octombrie. Ziua întâi. Tot în această zi, Cuviosul Roman, făcătorul de condace', in *Vieţile Sfinţilor pe luna octombrie*, retipărite și adăugite cu aprobarea Sfântului Sinod, după ediția din 1901-1911, Episcopia Romanului și Hușilor, 17-19;

[ANONYMUS], 'Pe 1 Octombrie, Sfânta Biserică face pomenirea Cuviosului Roman Melodul', in *Sinaxarul Mare al lunii Octombrie*, Constantin CHIRILA (ed.), translated from English by Maria Magdalena Vrânceanu, Doxologia, Iași 2015, 25-28;

[ANONYMUS], 'Romano il Melode', in *Testi mariani del primo millennio*, 1. Padri e altri autori greci, Georges GHARIB et alii (eds.), Città Nouva Editrice, Roma 2001, 694-730;

ALTANER, B., STUIBER, A., 'Romanus der Sänger (ὁ μελῳδός)', in *Patrologie. Leben, Schriften und Lehre der Kirchenväter*, Herder, Freiburg-Basel-Wien 1980, 532-533;

AVERINCEV, Sergej S., *L'anima e lo specchio. L'universo della poetica bizantina*, Introduzione all' edizione italiana di Pier Cesare Bori, Società editrice il Mulino, Bologna 1988;

BARDENHEWER, Otto, 'Romanus der Sänger', in *Patrologie*, Herdersche Verlagshandlung, Freiburg im Breisgau 1910, 486-487;

-, 'Romanus der Sänger', in *Geschichte der altkirchlichen Literatur*, vol. 5, Wissenschaftliche Buchgesellschaft, Darmstadt 1962, 159-165;

DI BERARDINO, Angelo, 'Romano il Melode', in *Patrologia, vol. 5: Dal Concilio di Calcedonia (451) a Giovanni Damasceno († 750)*, I Patri orientali, Institutum Patristicum Augustinianum, Casa Editrice Marietti, Genova 2000, 93-94;

> *English translation*: DI BERARDINO, Angelo, 'Romanus Melodus', in *Patrology: the Eastern Fathers from the Council of Chalcedon (451) to John of Damascus (+750)*, English translation by Adrian Walford, James Clarke&Co., Cambridge 2006, 100-102.

BOUVY, Edmond, 'Problème historique relatif a S. Romanus', in *Poètes et Mélodes. Étude sur les origines de rythme tonique dans l'hymnographie de l'Église grecque*, Impr. Lafare frères, Nimes 1886, 367-375;

BRANISTE, Ene, 'Condacul', in *Liturgica generală*, vol. 1, Eugen Drăgoi (ed.), Episcopia Dunării de Jos, Galaţi ³2002, 324-325;

BRECK, John, 'Roman Melodul: Condace', in *Cum citim Sfânta Scriptură. Despre structura limbajului biblic*, translated by Ioana Tămăian, Reîntregirea, Alba-Iulia 2005, 309-313;

CANTARELLA, Raffaele, 'Romano il Melode', in *Poeti Bizantini, volume secundo: Introduzione, traduzioni e commento*, Societa' Editrice 'Vita e Pensiero', Milano 1948, 106-112;

CAYRE, Fulbert, 'Romanos le Mélode', in *Précis de Patrologie et d'Histoire de la théologie*, vol. 2, Société de Saint Jean l'Evangéliste, Desclée et C-ie, éditeurs pontificaux, Paris-Tournai-Rome 1927-1930, 286-288 (²1955, 207-210);

> *Italian translation*: CAYRE, Fulberto, *Patrologia e storia della Teologia*, traduzione di D. Tebaldo Pellizzari, con una lettera di S.E. il Card. Elia Dalla Costa, Arcivescovo di Firenze, al traduttore, vol. 2, terzo e quarto libro, Società di S. Giovanni Evangelista, Roma 1938, 310-313.

COMAN, Ioan G., 'Roman Melodul', in *Patrologie*, Institutul Biblic şi de Misiune al Bisericii Ortodoxe Române, Bucureşti 1956, 297-298 (²1999, Sfânta Mânăstire Dervent 192-193);

ΔΕΤΟΡΑΚΗ, Θεοχάρη Ε., 'το κοντάκιο', in *Βυζαντινή θρησκευτική ποίηση και υμνογραφία*, εκδόσις β΄ με πρόσθηκες, Ρέθυμνο ²1997, 34-45;

-, 'Ρωμανός ο Μελωδός', in *Βυζαντινή θρησκευτική ποίηση και υμνογραφία ...*, 46-55;

-, 'Ρωμανός ο Μελωδός', in *Βυζαντινή Φιλολογία. Τα πρόσωπα και τα κείμενα*, vol. 2: από τον Ιουστινιανό έως τον Φώτιο (527-900), Ηρακλείο Κρήτης 2003, 131-163;

ΕΥΣΤΡΑΤΙΑΔΟΥ, Σωφρονίου, 'Ρωμανὸς μελῳδὸς', in *Ἁγιολόγιον τῆς Ὀρθοδόξου Ἐκκλησίας*, Ἐκδόσεις Ἀποστολικῆς Διακονίας τῆς Ἐκκλησίας τῆς Ἑλλάδος, Ἀθήνα 410;

ΦΑΝΟΥΡΓΑΚΗΣ, Βασίλειος Δ., 'Ρωμανὸς ὁ Μελωδός', in *Ἡ χριστιανική γραμματεία μετά τὸ 450*, Ἐκδόσεις Ὑπηρεσία Δημοσιευμάτων, Θεσσαλονίκη 1986, 107-110;

ΦΛΟΡΟΦΣΚΥ, Γεώργου, 'Ο Αγ. Ρωμανός', in *Οι βυζαντινοί Πατέρες του έκτου, εβδόμου και ογδόου αιώνα*, traducere de Παναγιώτου Κ. Παλλή, Εκδόσεις Π. Πουρναρά, Θεσσαλονίκη 2007, 23-24;

ΦΩΚΑΪΔΗΣ, Φωκάς Ν., 'Ε': Βυζαντινοί εκκλησιαστικοί συγγραφείς', in *Περί τήν ιεράν ασματικήν τέχνην των Ελλήνων: δοκιμία κριτικής*, Εκδόσεις Ελλήνων Φιλομούσων, Λευκωσία 1986, 81-83;

FRANK, Karl Suso, *Lehrbuch der Geschichte der Alten Kirche*, Mitarbeit: Dr. Elisabeth Grünbeck, 2. verbessserte Auflage 1997, Ferdinand Schöningh, Paderborn-München-Wien-Zürich 451;

GRILLMEIER, Alois, 'Zur konkreten Christologie: Die Mysterien des Lebens Jesu bei Romanos Melodos', in *Jesus der Christus im Glauben der Kirche*, vol. 2/2: Die Kirche von Konstantinopel im 6. Jahrhundert, Unter Mitarbeit von Therasia Hainthaler, Herder, Freiburg i. Br. 1989, 534-544;

> *English translation*: GRILLMEIER, Alois, 'Concrete christology: the mysteries of the life of Jesus in Romanos the Melodist', in *Christ in Christian Tradition*, vol. 2: From The Council of Chalcedon (451) to Gregory the Great (590-604), Part II: The Church of Constantinople in the sixth Century, translated by John Cawte&Pauline Allen, A Cassel imprint, Mowbray 1995, 513-523.

ΧΡΗΣΤΟΥ, Παναγιώτη Κ., 'Ρωμανός ο Μελωδός', in *Ελληνική Πατρολογία*, vol. 5, Πρωτοβυζαντινή περίοδος στ'-θ' αιώνες, Εκδοτικός Οίκος Κυρομάνος, Θεσσαλονίκη 1992, 599-617 (^{2}2006, 599-617);

-, 'Ρωμανός Μελωδός', in *Πατέρες και θεολόγοι του Χριστιανισμού*, Εκδοτικός Οίκος Κυρομάνος, Θεσσαλονίκη 1991, 349-354;

IMPELLIZERI, Salvatore, 'Roman Melodul', in *Literatura Bizanțului*, translated by Nicolae Șerban-Tanașoca, Univers, București 1971, 226-235;

IORDĂCHESCU, Cicerone, 'Poeți greci din veacurile VI, VII și VIII. Roman Melodul', in *Istoria vechii literaturi creștine*, vol. 3, Țerk&Caminschi, Iași 1935, 84-85 (^{2}1996, Moldova, Iași vol. 2, partea a III-a, 84-85);

KANNENGIESSER, Charles, 'Romanos the Melodist (d. 555/565)', in *Handbook of Patristic Exegesis. The Bible in Ancient Christianity*, Brill, Leiden-Boston 2006, 932-936;

KRUMBACHER, K., 'Romanos', in *Geschichte der Byzantinischen litteratur von Justinian bis zum Ende des oströmischen Reiches (527-1453)*, G.H. Beck'sche Verlagsbuchhandlung, München 1891, 312-318 (^{2}1897, 663-671);

LASCAROV-MOLDOVANU, Al., 'Cuviosul Roman, făcătorul de condace', in *Viețile Sfinților*, vol. 7, Artemis, București 1999, 16-20;

MAN, Ligia, 'Doctrina mariană în tradiția patristică. Declinul literaturii patristice, sec. VI-VIII. Sf. Roman Melodul († 560)', in *Mă vor ferici toate neamurile ... Elemente de mariologie biblică, patristică, magisterială*, Galaxia Gutenberg, Târgu-Lăpuș 2006, 165-166;

MCGUCKING, John Anthony, 'Romanos the Melodist', in *The Westminster Handbook to Patristic Theology*, John Knox Press, Louisville-London 2004, 297;

> *Romanian translation*: MCGUCKING, Pr. John Anthony, 'Roman Melodul', in *Dicționar de Teologie Patristică*, translated by Dragoș Dâscă and Alin-Bogdan Mihăilescu, col. 'Patristica. Studii', 13, Doxologia, Iași 2014, 431.

-, 'Poetry and hymnography (2): the Greek World', in *Oxford Handbook of Early Christian studies*, Susan ASHBROOK HARVEY and David C. HUNTER (eds.), Oxford University Press, Oxford 2008, 641-656;

ΜΗΤΣΑΚΗ, Καριοφίλη, 'Κοντάκιον', in *Ἡ βυζαντινὴ ὑμνογραφία ἀπὸ τὴν Καινὴ Διαθήκη ὡς τὴν εἰκονομαχία*, vol. 1, Ἐκδόσεις Πατριαρχικὸν Ἵδρυμα Πατερικῶν Μελετῶν, col. 'Χριστιανικὴ Γραμματολογία', 1, Θεσσαλονίκη 1971, 171-353;

-, 'Ῥωμανὸς ὁ Μελῳδός', in *Ἡ βυζαντινὴ ὑμνογραφία ἀπὸ τὴν Καινὴ Διαθήκη ...*, 357-509;

> *Review*: PASCHOS, P.B., 'Kariofilis Mitsakis, *Byzantine Hymnography*, v. I, *From the New Testament to the Iconoclast Controversy*, Thessaloniki, Patriarchal Institute of Patristic Studies, 1971, pp. 588, [History of

Christian Literature Series, No. 1]', *Balkan Studies*, vol. 16 (1975), 2, 244-250.

MORESCHINI, Claudio, NORELLI, Enrico, 'Romano il Melode', in *Storia della Letteratura Cristiana antica greca e latina*, vol. 2: Dal concilio di Nicea agli inizi del Medioevo, Morcelliana, Brescia 1996, 932-937;

> *Romanian translation*: MORESCHINI, Claudio, NORELLI, Enrico, 'Roman Melodul', in *Istoria literaturii creştine vechi greceşti şi latine*, vol. 2/2: De la Conciliul de la Niceea la începuturile Evului Mediu, translated by Hanibal Stănciulescu, Polirom, Iaşi 2004, 343-347;
> *German translation*: MORESCHINI, Claudio, NORELLI, Enrico, 'Romanus Melodus', in *Handbuch der Antiken Christlichen Literatur*, Gütersloher Verlagshaus, Gütersloh 2007, 625-626.

ΜΠΑΛΑΝΟΥ, Δημητρίου Σίμου, 'Ρωμανὸς ὁ μελῳδός', *Πατρολογία (οἱ ἐκκλησιαστικοί Πατέρες καὶ συγγραφείς τῶν ὀκτώ πρώτων αἰώνων)*, Ἀθήνα 1930, 553-559;

ΝΙΚΟΔΗΜΟΥ, Ἁγιορείτου, 'Τῇ αὐτῇ μνήμη τοῦ Ὁσίου Πατρὸς ἡμῶν Ῥωμανοῦ, τοῦ ποιητοῦ τῶν Κοντακίων', in *Συναξαριστὴς τῶν δώδεκα μηνῶν τοῦ ἐνιαυτοῦ*, vol. 1: περιέχων τοὺς τέσσαρας μῆνας Σεπτέμβριον, Ὀκτώβριον, Νοέμβριον, Δεκέμβριον, Ἐκδόσεις Δόμος, Ἀθήνα ²2005, 200-201;

OLD, Hughes Oliphant, 'Romanos the Melode (fl. ca. 540)', in *The Reading and Preaching of the Scriptures in the Worship of the Christian Church*, vol. 3: The Medieval Church, Wm. B. Eerdmans Publishing Co., Grand Rapids/Mich.-Cambridge 1999, 7-20;

PARRY, Ken, 'Romanos', in *The Wiley Blackwell Companion to Patristics*, Wiley Blackwell, Oxford 2015, 135-136;

ΤΩΜΑΔΑΚΗ, Νικολάου Β., 'Το πρόβλημα Ρωμανός', in *Ἡ βυζαντινὴ ὑμνογραφία καὶ ποίησις ἤτοι εἰσαγωγή εἰς τὴν βυζαντινὴ φιλολογίαν*, vol. 2, Ἐκδόσεις Π. Πουρναρᾶ, Θεσσαλονίκη ⁴1993, 81-181;

ΤΣΑΜΗ, Δημητρίου Γ., 'Ρωμανός ο Μελωδός', in *Εκκλησιαστική γραμματολογία*, Εκδόσεις Π. Πουρναρά, Θεσσαλονίκη 1985, 201-202;

VINTILESCU, Petre, 'Roman Melodul', in *Despre poezia imnografică din cărţile de ritual şi cântare bisericească*, Tipografia Cărţilor Bisericeşti, Bucureşti 1937, 71-78 (Renaşterea, Cluj-Napoca ²2005, 45-58);

VOICU, Constantin, DUMITRASCU, Nicu, 'Roman Melodul', in *Patrologie. Manual pentru Seminariile teologice*, Institutul Biblic şi de Misiune al Bisericii Ortodoxe Române, Bucureşti 2004, 225-230;

VOICU, Constantin, 'Roman Melodul', in *Patrologie şi literatură post-patristică*, vol. 3, Basilica, Bucureşti 2010, 117-121;

-,/COLDA, Lucian-Dumitru, *Patrologie şi literatură postpatristică*, vol. 3, *Basilica*, Bucureşti,2015, 188-192;

WELLESZ, Egon, 'Kontakion', in *A History of Byzantine Music and Hymnography*, Clarendon Press, Oxford ²1962, 179-197.

7. Studies&articles

ADAM, Domin, 'Înţelesul muzicii bisericeşti şi marii imnografi', *Altarul Reîntregirii*, vol. 1 (2009), 263-297 (about kontakion, 278-281; about Romanos the Melodist, 285-294);

ALEXIOU, Margaret, 'The Lament of the Virgin in Byzantine Literature and Modern Greek Folk-Song', *BMGS*, vol. 1 (1975), 111-140;

ALVETEG, Kristina, 'In Silence we Speak: Romanos Melodos and Mary at the Cross', *StPatr*, vol. 42 (2006), 279-284;

ΑΜΙΡΑΛΗ, Γεωργίου Νικ., '«Ρωμανοῦ αἶνος εἰς τό πάθος καὶ τήν Ἀνάστασιν». Ἑρμηνευτικὴ ἀνάλυση τοῦ Ὕμνου', *GrēgPal*, vol. 60 (1977), 112-121;

APOSTOL-CERNAVODA, Marin, 'Biruinţa – Condac de Sfântul Roman Melodul', *GBis*, 1 (1970), 1-6, 366-375;

ARCO MAGRI, M., 'Il canticum 55 M.-Tr. di Romano Melodi in alcuni codici Messinesi', Κοινωνία. *Rivista dell' Associazione di Studi Tardoantichi*, vol. 3 (1979), 113-141;

ARENTZEN, Thomas, '«Kom og ta del»! – Romanos' *Julehymne* og dens liturgiske kontekst', *NTT*, vol. 107 (2006), 2, 122-137;

-, 'Hør hva jeg er, for jeg er den du ser! Maria-fremstillinger i *Akathistos-hymnen* og Romanos' *Bebudelseshymne*', *SvTK*, vol. 87 (2011), 4, 162-168;

-, '«Your virginity shines» – The Attraction of the Virgin in the *Annunciation Hymn* by Romanos the Melodist', *StPatr*, vol. 68 (2013), 125-132;

-, 'Skjønnheten og skjøgen – Romanos' hymne om synderinnen som salver Jesus', in *Skjønnhet og tilbedelse*, Svein RISE/ Knut-Willy SÆTHER (eds.), Akademika Forlag, Trondheim 2013, 145-160;

-, 'Kjødets teologi – Romanos Meloden', *Gud er alltid større: Kirkefedrenes teologiske språk*, 2015, 223-239;

-, 'Voices Interwoven: Refrens and Vocal Participation in the Kontakia', *JÖB*, vol. 66 (2016), 1-10;

-, KRUEGER, Derek, 'Romanos in Manuscript: Some Observation on the Patmos Kontakarion', in *Proceedings of the 23rd International Congress of Byzantine Studies, Belgrade, 22-27 August 2016: Round Table*, Bojana KRSMANOVIĆ/Ljubomir MILANOVIĆ (eds.), Belgrade 2016, 648-654.

-, 'Struggling with Romanos's Dagger of Taste', in *Knowing Bodies, Passionate Souls. Sense Perceptions in Byzantium*, Susan ASHBROOK HARVEY/Margaret MULLETT (eds.), Dumbarton Oaks Research Library and Collection, Harvard 2017, 169-182;

ARGARATE, P., '«Tu vedi e stringi colui che i cherubini non possono guardare». La madre di Dio nei Kontakia di Natale di Romano il Melode', in *Motivi e forme della poesia cristiana antica tra Scrittura e tradizione classica*, XXXVI Incontro di studiosi dell'antichità cristiana, Roma, 3-5 maggio 2007, Parte seconda, *SEAug*, 108, Institutum Patristicum Augustinianum, Roma 2008, 807-820;

ASLANOV, Cyril, 'Romanos the Melodist and Palestinian *Piyyut*: Sociolinguistic and Pragmatic Perspectives', in *Jews in Byzantium. Dialectics of Minority and Majority Cultures*, Robert BONFIL et alii (eds.), col. 'Jerusalem Studies in Religion and Culture', 14, Brill, Leiden-Boston 2012, 613-628;

ASMUS, M.B., 'Творчество Романа Сладкопевца', *Весник Российского гуманитарного научного фонда*, 2000, 189-200;

AVERINCEV, S., 'Romanos the Melode', *Kultura Vizantii*, vol. 1 (1984), 318-327;

-, 'K ponimaniju poetiki Romana Sladkopevca', *Actes du XIVe Congrès International d'Étude Byzantines*, vol. 3, Academia Republicii Socialiste România, Bucureşti 1976, 699-705;

BANDY, Anastasius C., '*Addenda et Corrigenda* to M. Carpenter, «Kontakia of Romanos, Byzantine Melodist», Volume I: On the Person of Christ, Vol. II: On the Christian Life. Volume I [Part I]', *ByS(P)*, vol. 2 (1975), 139-182; vol. 3 (1976), 64-113 (part II);

-, '*Addenda et Corrigenda* to Carpenter, M. *Kontakia of Romanos, Byzantine Melodist*, Vol. 2: On the Christian Life, Part 1', *ByS(P)*, vol. 7 (1980), 78-113, 221-260 (part II);

BARKHUIZEN, J.H., 'Narrative Apostrophe in the Kontakia of Romanos the Melodist with Special Reference to his Hymn on Judas', *ACl*, vol. 29 (1986), 19-27;

-, 'Romanos Melodos: Essay on the Poetics of his Kontakion «Resurrection of Christ» (Maas-Trypanis 24)', *ByZ*, vol. 79 (1986), 1, 17-28 (part I) and 2, 268-281 (part II);

-, 'Narrative The Speaker in the Hymns of Romanos the Melodist', *EkklPh*, vol. 68-69 (1986-1987), 102-111;

-, 'Association of Ideas as a Principle of Composition in Romanos', *Hell.*, vol. 39 (1988), 1, 18-24;

-, 'Romanos Melodos and the Composition of his Hymns: Prooimion and Final Strophe', *Hell.*, vol. 40 (1989), 1, 62-77;

-, 'Romanos and the Nika Riots (532AD): a Religious Perspective', *EkklPh*, NS, vol. 1 (1990), 30-39;

-, 'Romanos Melodos, On the Temptation of Joseph: a study on his use of imagery', *Acta Patristica et Byzantina*, vol. 1 (1990), 1, 1-31;
-, 'Romanos' Encomium on Joseph: Portrait of an Athlete', *JÖB*, vol. 40 (1990), 91-106;
-, 'Romanos Melodos. Kontakion 10 (Oxf.) «On the Sinful Woman»', *ACl*, vol. 33 (1990), 33-52;
-, 'An Analysis of the Form and Content of Prayer as Liturgical Component in the Hymns of Romanos the Melodist', *EkklPh*, NS, vol. 2 (1991), 91-102;
-, 'The «New Song» as Traditional Biblical and Patristic Motif in Romanos the Melodist', *Hell.*, vol. 42 (1991-1992), 1, 157-162;
-, 'Romanos the Melodist, Kontakion 55SC: a prayer of penitence', *EkklPh*, NS, vol. 3 (1992), 107-121;
-, 'Christ as metaphor in the hymns of Romanos the Melodist', *Acta Patristica et Byzantina*, vol. 2 (1991), 1, 1-15 (part I) and vol. 3 (1992), 1, 1-14 (part II);
-, 'Romanos Melodos «On the ten virgins» (48Oxf.=51SC)', *ACl*, vol. 36 (1993), 39-54;
-, 'Romanos Melodos. On Repentance (Oxf. 52:8bSC)', *EkklPh*, NS, vol. 4 (1993), 43-53;
-, 'Lazarus in the Tomb and the Topos of the Lament of Hades', *EkklPh*, NS, vol. 5 (1994), 83-105;
-, 'The Reconstitution and Reanimation of Lazarus in the Preaching of the Early Church', *EkklPh*, NS, vol. 5 (1994), 109-124;
-, 'Romanos Melodos: On Earthquakes and Fires', *JÖB*, vol. 45 (1995), 1-18;
-, 'The Parable of the Prodigal Son as a Eucharistic *Metaphor in Romanos Melodos' Kontakion 49 (Oxf.)*', *ACl*, vol. 39 (1996), 39-54;
-, 'Romanos Melodos, verse homily «On the leper»', *Acta Patristica et Byzantina*, vol. 8 (1997), 26-41;
-, 'Thomas – Portrait of an Apostle: Proclus Constantinopolitanus and Romanus Melodus', *Acta Patristica et Byzantina*, vol. 15 (2004), 22-37;

-, 'Romanos Melodos: Kontakion 8 «On the tree children»', *Acta patristica et byzantina*, vol. 16 (2005), 1-28;
-, 'Romanos Melodos, «On the Massacre of the Innocents»: A Perspective on *Ekphrasis* ad a Method of Patristic Exegesis', *ACl*, vol. 50 (2007), 1, 29-50;
BARNEA, Alexăndrel, 'Condacul Naşterii', *TV*, 3 (1993), 11-12, 15-30;
BASILIKOPOULOS, A., 'Ῥωμανικὰ Σύμμεικτα. Α. Παρατηρήσεις καὶ ἐπανορθώσεις εἰς τὸν ΚΣΤ ὕμνον', *Athēna*, 59 (1955), 78-80;
BAUD-BOVY, Samuel, 'Sur un prélude de Romanos', *Byz*, vol. 13 (1938), 1, 217-226;
-, 'Sur un «Sacrifice d'Abraham» de Romanos et sur l'existence d'un théatre religieux à Byzance', *Byz*, vol. 13 (1938), 1, 321-334;
BELEAN, Nicolae, 'Elemente de mariologie şi antropologie soteriologică în creaţia imnografică a Sfântului Roman Melodul', *Teologia*, 9 (2005), 2, 38-47;
BERKOWITZ, Luci, 'Observations on rare words in the vocabulary of Romanus Melodus', *Glotta*, vol. 73 (1995-1996), 1, 118-126;
BICKERSTETH, E., 'A Source of Romanos' Contakion on the Hypapante', *Actes du VIe Congrès International d'Études Byzantines*, vol. 1, École des Hautes Études, Paris 1950, 375-381;
ΒΟΥΛΙΣΜΑΣ, Ε., 'Περὶ ἐκκλησιαστικῶν μελῳδῶν', *EkklAl*, 12 (1893), 45, 358-361;
BOUSQUET, R., 'Le culte de Saint Romain le Mélode dans l'Église grecque et l'Église arménienne', *EOr*, vol. 3 (1899-1900), 3, 339-342;
BROCK, Sebastian, 'From Ephrem to Romanos', *StPatr*, vol. 20 (1989), 139-151 (republished in: BROCK, Sebastian, *From Ephraem to Romanos. Interactions between Syriac and Greek in Late Antiquity*, col. 'Variorum Collected Studies Series', 664, Aldershot, Ashgate 1999, 139-151);
BRUNNER, Theodore F., 'P. Amst. I 24: A Romanus Melodus Papyrus', *ZPE*, vol. 96 (1993), 185-189;

BUNTA, Silviu, 'Sfântul Roman Melodul: Condacul la Naşterea lui Hristos', *Revista Teologică*, 7 (1997), 1-4, 146-153;

BUSSAGLI, Marco, 'Sul contacio della Natività di Romano il Melodo. A proposito dell' angelo-stella', *RSBN*, NS, vol. 22-23 (1985-1986), 3-49;

-, 'Ancora sul contacio della Natività di Romano il Melodo: una nota', *RSBN*, NS, vol. 24 (1987), 3-6;

CAMMELLI, G., 'L'inno per la Natività di Romano il Melode', *Studii Bizantini*, vol. 1 (1925), 45-58;

CAMERON, A., 'The Theotokos in Sixth-Century Constantinople', *JThS*, NS, vol. 29 (1978), 79-108;

CARPENTER, Marjorie, 'Krumbacher's metrical theory applied to the Christmas Hymn of Romanos', *TPAPA*, vol. 58 (1927), 123-131;

-, 'The Paper that Romanos Swallowed', *Spec.*, vol. 7 (1932), 1, 3-22;

CATTANEO, Enrico, 'Poesia e teologia in Romano il Melodo', *RdT*, vol. 45 (2004), 2, 296-307;

CÂNDEA, Virgil, 'Despre condacul Naşterii Domnului', *StTeol*, 45 (1993), 5-6, 26-33;

CHEVALIER, Célestin, 'Mariologie de Romanos (490-550 environ), le roi de Mélodes', *RSR*, vol. 28 (1938), 1, 48-71;

COLACLIDES, P., 'Critical Note on a Line of Romanos', *ByZ*, vol. 61 (1968), 1, 268-269;

CONCA, F., 'Giuseppe e la moglie di Putifarre (Romano il Melode, contacio 44 M-T)', in *Contributi di filologia greca*, Italo GALLO (ed.), Quaderni del Dip. di Scienze dell'Antichità del l'Univ. degli Studi di Salerno 6, Arte Tipografica, Napoli 1990, 143-148;

COUNTRYMAN, L. William, 'A Monothelite Kontakion of the Seventh Century', *GOTR*, vol. 19 (1974), 1, 23-36;

-, 'A sixth-century plea against religious violence: Romanos on Elijah', in *Reading Religions in the Ancient World: Essays presented to Robert McQueen Grant on his 90th birthday*, David E. AUNE, Robin Darling YOUNG (eds.), *NT.S*, 125, Brill, Leiden-Boston 2007, 289-301;

CRĂCIUN, Casian, 'Naşterea Domnului în imnele Sfântului Roman Melodul', *MitrArd*, 30 (1985), 11-12, 11-12 (republished in: CRĂCIUN, Casian, *Poarta Cerului*, Episcopia Dunării de Jos, Galaţi 1999, 145-149);

CRESCI, Lia Raffaella, 'Analisi di alcune strutture compositive di Romano il Melodo', Κοινωνία, vol. 30-31 (2006-2007), 2, 169-175;

-, 'Didascalie mimetiche nei Contaci di Romano il Melodo', *Byz*, vol. 77 (2007), 1, 64-86;

-, 'Il rapporto tra efimnio e strofe nei Contaci di Romano il Melodo', in *Motivi e forme della poesia cristiana antica tra Scrittura e tradizione classica*, XXXVI Incontro di studiosi dell'antichità cristiana, Roma, 3-5 maggio 2007, Parte seconda, *SEAug*, 108, Institutum Patristicum Augustinianum, Roma 795-805;

-,/MARZI, Valeria, 'Elementi innodici nei Contaci di Romano il Melodo', *Paideia. Rivista di filologia, ermeneutica e critica letteraria*, vol. 66 (2011), 53-82;

-, 'Teologia e retorica nei *Contaci* di Romano il Melodo', in *La Teologia dal V all' VIII Secolo fra Sviluppo e Crisi*, XLI Incontro di Studiosi dell'Antichità Cristiana, Roma, 9-11 maggio 2013, *SEAug*, 140, Institutum Patristicum Augustinianum, Roma, 2014, 725-737;

CUNNINGHAM, Mary B., 'The Reception of Romanos in Middle Byzantine Homiletics and hymnography', *DOP*, vol. 62 (2008), 251-260;

DAL COVOLO, Enrico, 'Maria contempla il mistero del Figlio. *Gli Inni di Natale di Efrem Siro e di Romano il Melòde*', in *Maria guida sicura in un mondo che cambia*, E.M. TONIOLO (ed.), Fine d' anno con Maria 22, Centro di Cultura Mariana 'Madre della Chiesa', Roma 2002, 65-88;

DALMAIS, Irénée-Henri, 'Imagerie syrienne et symbolisme hellénique dans les hymnes bibliques de Romanos le Mélode', *StPatr*, vol. 11 (1972), 22-26;

-, 'Tropaire, Kontakion, Canon. Les éléments constitutifs de l'hymnographie byzantine', in *Liturgie und Dichtung. Ein interdis-*

ziplanäres Kompendium, I (Historische Präsentation), H. BECKER, R. KACZYNSKI (eds.), EOS, St. Ottilien 1983, 421-434;
-, 'Hymnodie et Catéchèse: Mimre, madrashe, kontakia', in *L'Hymnographie: Conférences Saint-Serge*, 46ᵉ Semaine d'Etudes Liturgiques (juin 1999), A.M. TRIACCA et A. PISTOIA (eds.), Edizioni Liturgiche, Roma 2000, 171-177;
DE BOOR, G., 'Die Lebenszeit des Dichters Romanos', *ByZ*, vol. 9 (1900), 3, 633-640;

> Review: VAILHÉ, S., 'C. de Boor: *Die Lebenszeit des dichters Romanos* dans la *Byzantinische Zeitschrift*, 4 helt (1900), p. 633-640', *EOr*, vol. 4 (1901), 5, 313-314.

DEBÓRSKI, B., 'Maryja – Matka Odkupiciela – w poezji sw. Romana Slodkopiewcy', in *Matka Odkupiciela*, K. WIELICZKO (ed.), Lublin 2006, 71-86;
-, 'Maryja w kontakionie św. Romana Slodkopiewcy na Ofiarowanie Pana Jezusa w świątyni', in *Miłosierdzie, Kościół, Maryja. W hołdzie ojcu Profesorowi Zachariaszowi Jabłońskiemu, Paulinowi, Człowiekowi Kościoła, oddanemu Maryi*, Jasna Góra-Kraków-Szdłówek 2016, 63-81;
ΔΕΔΟΥΣΗΣ, Β.Σ., 'Ὁ ποιητὴς καὶ τὸ μέτρον τοῦ κοντακίου τῶν χαιρετισμῶν τῆς Παναγίας', *GrēgPal*, vol. 35 (1952), 147-155;
DELEHAYE, H., 'Saint Romanos le Mélode', *AnBoll*, vol. 13 (1894), 440-442;
ΔΕΤΟΡΑΚΗ, Θεοχάρους Ε., 'Ῥωμανικαὶ ἐπιδράσεις εἰς τὴν ποίησιν Κοσμᾶ τοῦ Μελωδοῦ', *EEBS*, vol. 44 (1979-1980), 223-230 (re-published in: Θεοχάρους Ε. ΔΕΤΟΡΑΚΗ, *Ῥωμανικαὶ ἐπιδράσεις εἰς τὴν ποίησιν Κοσμᾶ τοῦ Μελωδοῦ*, ἀνατυπόσης ἐκ του μδ', 1979-1980, τόμου τῆς Ἐπετηρίδος τῆς Ἑταιρείας Βυζαντινῶν Σπουδῶν, Τυπογραφείον Εμμ. Παπδάκη, Ἀθήνα, 1980; ²1997, ΔΕΤΟΡΑΚΗ, Θεοχάρους, *Βυζαντινὴ ὑμνογραφία. Πανεπιστημιακές παραδόσεις*, Ἡράκλειο, 199-207);
DMITRIEBITS-USPENSKY, N., 'Ὁ Ρωμανός ὁ Μελοδός ἦταν μόνο Μελωδός;', *EEThS*, vol. 26 (1981), 579-594;

DOBROV, Gregory W., 'A Dialogue with Death: Ritual Lament and the θρῆνος Θεοτόκου of Romanos Melodos', *GRBS*, vol. 35 (1994), 1, 385-405;

DONADEO, Maria, 'Romano il Melode: un santo d' Oriente del VI secolo', *EphMar*, vol. 35 (1985), 1-2, 197-200;

DOSTAL, Ant., 'Romanos le Mélode en traduction slavonne', *Byz(T)*, vol. 5 (1973), 87-98;

DŹWIGAŁA, Katarzyna Maria, 'Romanos the Melodist as a Teacher of the People in the Struggle Against Heresies', *Vox Patrum*, vol. 68 (2017), 37, 513-521;

-, 'Wyobraźnia i zmysły w nabożeństwie bizantyjskim w VI w. na przykładzie hymnów Romana Melodosa', *Liturgia Sacra*, 22 (2016), 2 (48), 499-511;

ΕΛΥΤΗΣ, Ὀδυσσέας, 'Ῥωμανός ὁ Μελωδός', in *Ἐν λευκῷ*, Ἐκδόσεις Ἴκαρος, ³2011, 35-56;

ÉMEREAU, Casimir, 'Mélanges des philologie byzantine', *EOr*, vol. 20 (1921), 123, 295-300 (part III: 'Les oeuvres de saint Romanos le Mélode', 299-300);

-, 'Hymnography Byzantini quorum nomina in litteras digessit notulisque adornavit (Continuatur)', *EOr*, vol. 24 (1925), 138, 163-179 ['Romanus Melodus (Ῥωμανός ὁ Μελῳδός)', 169-172];

ENACHE, Laura, 'Sfântul Roman Melodul', *TV*, NS, 15 (2005), 7-12, 40-53;

ERBICEANU, G., 'Imnologia epocii până la Damascen', *BORom*, 7 (1883), 3, 139-140 (only about Romanos the Melodist);

ERIKSEN, Uffe Holmsgaard, 'The Poet in the Pulpit: Drama and Rhetoric in the *kontakion* «On the Victory of the Cross» by Romanos Melodos', *Transfiguration. Nordic Journal of Religion and the Arts*, 2010/2011, 103-123;

-, 'Med Romanos Melodos I Byzans. *Refleksioner fra et ophold ved Det Svenske Institut I Istanbul*', *Dragomanen*, 18 (2016), 91-100;

ΕΥΣΤΡΑΤΙΑΔΗΣ, Σωφρονίου, 'Ῥωμανός ὁ Μελῳδός καί ἡ Ἀκάθιστος', *GrēgPal*, vol. 1 (1917), 193-207, 269-280, 625-634, 641-649, 817-832;

-, 'Ταμεῖον ἐκκλησιαστικῆς ποιήσεως', *EkklPh*, vol. 36 (1937), 490-492;

-, 'Ῥωμανὸς ὁ Μελῳδὸς καὶ τὰ ποιητικὰ αὐτοῦ ἔργα', *EEBS*, vol. 15 (1939), 182-255 (part I), 16 (1955), 210-283 (part II);

FARCAŞIU, Lucian, 'Sfântul imnograf Roman Melodul. Elemente de biografie şi opera sa imnografică', *Teologia*, 13 (2009), 1, 115-124;

FĂRCAŞ, Ioan-Irineu, '«Prunc tânăr, Dumnezeu Cel mai înainte de veci». Condacul Naşterii Domnului al cuviosului Roman Melodul', *Perspective. Revista Misiunii Române Unite cu Germania*, 29 (2007), 78, 19-31 (Romanian translation), 32-45 (German translation);

FERRARA, A., 'The Theology Found in the Akathistos Hymn', *Diakonia*, vol. 14 (1979), 12-18;

ΦΥΤΡΑΚΗΣ, Ἀνδρέας, 'Ῥωμανὸς ὡς μελῳδὸς κατὰ τοὺς ὕμνους τῆς Ἐκκλησίας', *Ὁ Ποιμήν*, vol. 3 (1935), 266-268;

-, 'Μέτρον καὶ μελῳδίαι εἰς τὴν ἐκκλησιαστικήν μας ποίησιν', *Ἐκκλησία*, 24, 15 Δεκεμβρίου 1983, 596-599;

FLETCHER, R.A., 'Three Early Byzantine Hymns and their place in the Liturgy of the church of Constantinopole', *ByZ*, vol. 51 (1958), 53-65;

FLOROS, C., 'Fragen zum musikalischen und metrischen Aufbau der Kontakion', *Actes du XIIe Congrès International d'Études Byzantines*, vol. 2, Comité Yougoslave des Études Byzantines, Belgrad 1964, 563-569;

FOLLIERI, Enrica, 'La catechesi ecclesiologica di Romano il Melode', in *Ecclesiologia e catechesi patristica 'Sentirsi Chiesa'*, Convegno di studio e aggiornamento Pontificium Institutum Altioris Latinitatis (Facoltà di Lettere cristiane e classiche), Roma, 6-7 marzo 1981, Sergio FELICI (ed.), Las, Roma 1982, 241-253;

FRANK, Georgia, 'Dialogue and Deliberation: the Sensory Self in the Hymns of Romanos the Melodist', in *Religion and the Self in Antiquity*, D. BRAKKE et alii (eds.), Indiana University Press, Bloomington 2005, 163-179;

-, 'Romanos and the Night Vigil in the Sixth Century', in *A People's History of Christianity*, vol. 3: *Byzantine Christianity*, Derek

KRUEGER (ed.), Augsburg Fortress Publishers, Minneapolis 2006, 59-78;
-, 'Memory and Forgetting in Romanos the Melodist's On the Newly Baptized', in *Between Personal and Institutional Religion. Self, Doctrine, and Practice in Late Antique Eastern Christianity*, Brouria BITTON-ASHKELONY/Lorenzo PERRONE (eds.), Cultural Encounters in Late Antiquity and the Middle Ages, Turnhout 2013, 37-55;
GADOR-WHITE, Sarah, 'Emotional Preaching: *Ekphrasis* in the *Kontakia* of Romanos', *Australasian Society for Classical Studies*, 31 (2010) [http://msc.uwa.edu.au/classics/ascs31];
-, 'Self-construction: Auto-*Ethopoeia* in Romanos' *Kontakia*', *Melbourne Historical Journal*, vol. 39 (2011), 2, 23-37;
-, 'Changing Conceptions of Mary in Sixth-Century Byzantium: The Kontakia of Romanos the Melodist', in *Questions of Gender in Byzantine Society*, Bronwen NEIL and Lynda GARLAND (eds.), Farnham, Ashgate 2013, 77-92;
-, 'Playing with Genre: Romanos the Melodist and his *Kontakion*', in *Approaches to Genre in the Ancient World*, Michelle BORG and Graeme MILES (eds.), Newcastle upon Tyne 2013, 159-175;
GAL, Dan, 'Sfântul Roman Melodul, autor al Condacului Crăciunului', *Legea Românească*, NS, 17 (2006), 4, 59-60;
GASSISI, S., 'Un antichissimo «kontakion» inedito. Saggio di testi liturgici', *ReO*, vol. 1 (1910-1911), 165-187;
GATIER, Pierre-Louis, 'Un séisme élément de datation de l'oeuvre de Romanos le Mélode', *JS*, 1-3 (1983), 229-238;
ΓΕΟΡΓΙΑΔΗΣ, Η., 'Ῥωμανὸς ὁ Μελῳδός', *Νέος Ποιμήν*, vol. 2 (1920), 529-544;
GROSDIDIER DE MATONS, José, 'L' isosyllabe et l'homotonie chez Romanos le Mélode', *Actes du XIe Congrès International d'Études Byzantines*, Munich, 1960, 200-205;
-, 'Le Kontakion', in *Gattungen der Musik in Einzeldarstellungen. Gedenkschrift Leo Schrade*, Wulf ARLT et alii (eds.), vol. 1, Erste Folge, Bern-München 1973, 245-268;

-, 'Kontakion et Canon: Piété popoulaire et liturgie officielle à Byzance', *Aug.*, vol. 20 (1980), 1-2, 191-203;

-, 'Liturgie et hymnopraphie: Kontakion et Canon', *DOP*, vol. 34-35 (1980-1981), 31-43;

-, 'Tradition et nouveauté dans la poésie byzantine', *BAGB*, 33 (1981), 64-80;

-, 'Aux origines de l'hymnographie byzantine, Romanos le Mélode et le Kontakion', in *Liturgie und Dichtung. Ein interdisziplanäres Kompendium*, H. BECKER, R. KACZYNSKI (eds.), I (Historische Präsentation), EOS, St. Ottilien 1983, 435-463;

GUEVIN, Benedict M., 'Dialogue between Death and the Devin in Saint Ephrem the Syrian and Saint Romanos the Melodist', *StPatr*, vol. 92 (2017), 113-118;

GUGGENBERGER, Rainer, 'Romanos Melod und Sein Verhältnis zu Weltlichen Autoritäten', *Estudos Linguísticos e literários*, 55 (2016), 94-119;

GUILLAUME, Chanoine L., 'Romanos le Mélode', in *Mélanges Godefroid Kurt*, vol. 2: Mémoires littérares, philologiques et archéologiques, Vaillant-Carmanne&Honoré Champion, Liege-Paris 1908, 83-93;

HANNICK, Christian, 'Zur Metrik des Kontakion', in *Byzantios, Fetschrift für Herbert Hunger zum 70. Geburtstag*, W. HÖRANDNER et alii (eds.), Ernst Becvar, Wien 1984, 107-119;

-, 'Le kontakion dans l'histoire de la musique ecclesiastique byzantine', *OS*, vol. 58 (2009), 1, 57-66;

HARVEY, Susan, 'Sensing More in Ancient Religion', *SvTK*, vol. 89 (2013), 3-4, 97-106 (about Romanos, 104-106);

HESZEN, Agnieszka, 'Methodius of Olympus – one of the Greek sources of Kontakia by Romanos the Melodist', *Classica Cracoviensia*, vol. 16 (2003), 63-79;

-, 'The sinful woman as an example of metanoia in Byzantine poetry', *Classica Cracoviensia*, vol. 17 (2014), 69-87;

ΧΡΗΣΤΟΥ, Παναγιώτου, 'Ἡ γένεσις τοῦ Κοντακίου', *Kl.*, vol. 6 (1974), 2, 273-350 (republished in: ΧΡΗΣΤΟΥ, Παναγιώτου,

Θεολογικά μελετήματα. *4. Υμνογραφία*, Πατριαρχικόν Ἵδρυμα Πατερικῶν Μελετῶν, Θεσσαλονίκη 1981, 137-227);

DE HALLEUX, André, 'Hellénisme er syrianité de Romanos le Mélode (A propos d'un ouvrage récente)', *RHE*, vol. 73 (1978), 3-4, 632-641;

HUNGER, Herbert, 'Romani il Melode – poeta, predicatore, retore – ed il suo publico', *RöHM*, vol. 25 (1983), 305-332 (German translation: HUNGER, Herbert, 'Romanos Melodos. Dichter, Prediger, Rhetor und sein Publikum', *JÖB*, vol. 34 (1984), 15-42);

-, 'Das lebenspendende Wasser. *Romanos Melodos, Kontakion 9 (Oxf. = 19 SC): Jesus und die Samariterin*', *JÖB*, vol. 38 (1988), 125-157;

-, 'Additamenta zu Romanos Melodos', in *Synodia Studia humanitatis Antonio Garzya septuagenario*, Ugo CRISCUOLO et alii (eds.), Napoli, 1997, 443-457;

-, 'Der Refrain in den Kontakia des Romanos Melodos. Vielfalt in der Einheit', in *Lesarten (Festschrift fuer Athanasios Kambylis zum 70. Geburtstag)*, Athanasios KAMBYLIS et alii (eds.), W. de Gruyter, Berlin-New York 1998, 53-60;

-, 'Romanos Melodos. Überlegungen zum Ort und zur Art des Vortrages seiner Hymnen. Mit anschließender kurzer Strukturanalyse eines Kontakions (O 19. SC 35 = Maria unter dem Kreuz)', *ByZ*, vol. 92 (1999), 1, 1-9;

-, 'Romanos Melodos, Kontakion über die Auferweckung des Lazarus I (Samstag vor Palmsonntag; Maas-Trypanis Nr. 14; Grosdidier de Matons Nr. 26)', in *Λιθόστρωτον. Studien zur byzantinischen Kunst und Geschichte. Festschrift für Marcell Restle*, Birgitt BORKOPP/Thomas STEPPAN (eds.), Anton Hiersemann, Stuttgart 2000, 117-124;

IACOBESCU, Petru, 'Troparul și condacul sărbătorii Nașterii Domnului', *MitrBan*, 6 (1956), 10-12, 181-183;

IONESCU, Răzvan, 'Literatura dramatică în Bizanț', *TV*, NS, 17 (2007), 7-12, 16-30;

IORGA, Alexandru, 'Jesus Christ – The divine Healer and Savior in Kontakia Written by Romanos the Melodist', in *Orientalia Patristica. Papers of the International Patristic Symposium*, May 1-4, 2017, Didahia Severin Publishing, Drobeta-Turnu-Severin 2018, 280-289 (Romanian translation: 'Iisus Hristos – Medicul divin și activitatea Sa în condacele Sfântului Roman Melodul', in *Orientalia Patristica ...*, 583-593);

JOHANSEN, Johannes, 'Romanos Melodos – dramaturgen på Konstantinopels prekestol', in *Ortodokse røster i Nord: en antologi*, Johannes JOHANSEN (ed.), Hl. Silouan, Lyngby 2003, 133-143;

KAMBYLIS, A., 'Bemerkungen zum Text des Romanos', *ByZ*, vol. 64 (1971), 1, 28-32;

KHAWAM, Réne R., 'Le mystère de l'Epiphanie. Célébrations paraliturgique par Romanos le Mélode (VIe siècle)', *VS*, vol. 92 (1955), 41-63;

KIRCH, Konrad, 'Eine neun Ansicht über die Metrik des Romanos', *ByZ*, vol. 9 (1900), 2, 453-463;

ΚΟΜΙΝΗ, Ἀθανασίου, 'Πηγαὶ τοῦ εἰς τὸν νιπτῆρα ὕμνου Ῥωμανοῦ τοῦ Μελῳδοῦ', *EEBS*, vol. 27 (1957), 224-232;

ΚΟΡΑΚΙΔΗ, Ἀλεξάνδρου Σ., *Τό ὅραμα τοῦ Ῥωμανοῦ τοῦ Μελῳδοῦ*, Ἀποστολικὴ Διακονία, Ἀθῆναι 1972 (republished in:

-, *Τὰ περί τοῦ Ῥωμανοῦ τοῦ Μελῳδοῦ μελετήματα*, ἔκδοσις συμπληρωμένη, Ἐκδόσεις Π. Πουρναρᾶς, Θεσσαλονίκη 2002, 283-320);

-, 'Ὁ Ῥωμανός ὁ Μελῳδός ὁ ποιητής τῶν κοντακίων', *Κοινωνία*, 3 (2010), 233-244;

KOSKENNIEMI, Erkki, 'Back to the Paradise: Adam and Eve in Romanos Melodos', in *Adam and Eve Story in Jewish, Christian and Islamic Perspectives*, Antti LAATO and Lotta VALVE (eds.), col. 'Studies in the Reception History of the Bible', 8, Åbo Akademi University, Eisenbrauns 2017, 199-215;

ΚΟΥΡΕΜΠΕΛΕΣ, Ἰωάννης, 'Τό ἀνώνυμο κοντάκιο «Εἰς ἁγίους Πατέρας»: Ἕνα μονοθελητικό κοντάκιο τοῦ 7^{ου} αἰώνα ἤ ἕνα κοντάκιο τοῦ Ῥωμανοῦ τοῦ Μελῳδοῦ;', *GrēgPal*, 82 (1999), 47-

135 [republished in: Ι.Γ. ΚΟΥΡΕΜΕΛΕΣ, *Οἰκουμενικά παραδείγματα στήν ἱστορία τῆς Ἐκκλησίας*, vol. 1, Ἐκδόσεις Π. Πουρναρᾶ, Θεσσαλονίκη 2002, 101-225 (^{2}2010, 104-230)];

> *Review*: PRELIPCEAN, Alexandru, 'Ιωάννης Γ. Κουρεμπελές, *Οἰκουμενικά παραδείγματα στήν ἱστορία τῆς Ἐκκλησίας*, τόμος Α', Ἐκδόσεις Π. Πουρναρᾶ, Θεσσαλονίκη, ^{2}2010, 301σσ. [Ioannis G. Kourempeles, *Modele ecumenice în istoria Bisericii*, vol. 1, Ed. P. Pournaras, Tesalonic, ^{2}2010, 301 pp.]', *StTeol*, NS, 8 (2012), 1, 266-270.

-, 'Ἡ χρήση τοῦ ὅρου «φύσις» ἀπό τόν Ρωμανό τόν Μελωδό καί ἡ ἀντιαιρετική της προοπτική', *EEThS*, NS, vol. 13 (2003), 171-195 [republished in: ΚΟΥΡΕΜΠΕΛΕΣ, Ιωάννης, *Ρωμανοῦ Μελῳδοῦ θεολογική δόξα* …, 103-142 (^{2}2010, 103-142); French translation: KOUREMBELES, Ioannis, 'Les expressions christologiques «double par nature» et «Christ invincible dans la nature vaincue» de Romanos le Mélode par rapport à leur perspective antihérétique', *OrthFor*, vol. 19 (2005), 1-2, 96-107;

-, *Ost- und Westerweiterung in Theologie. 20 Jahre Orthodoxe Theologie in München*, Th. NIKOLAOU et alii (eds.), EOS, St. Ottilien 2006, 95-107];

-, 'Ἡ θεολογία τοῦ Ἀκαθίστου ὕμνου', in *Εἰσηγήσεις μαθημάτων θεολογικοῦ κύκλου «Ἀνοιχτοῦ Πανεπιστημίου» τοῦ Δήμου Θεσσαλονίκης*, Χ. ΚΡΙΚΩΝΗΣ (ed.), Θεσσαλονίκη, 2004, 171-202 [republished in: ΚΟΥΡΕΜΠΕΛΕΣ, Ιωάννης, *Ρωμανοῦ Μελῳδοῦ θεολογική δόξα* …, 143-208 (^{2}2010, 143-208); German translation: 'Die Theologie des Hymnus Akathistos und seine ökumenische Bedeutung', in *Auf der Suche nach der Seele Europas – Marienfrömmigkeit in Ost und West*, Studientagung der Pro Oriente-Sektion Salzburg aus Anlass ihres 20jährigen Bestehens, 7. und 8. Oktober 2005, Peter Leander HOFRICHTER (ed.), col. 'Pro Oriente', 30, Tyrolia, Innsbruck-Wien, 2007, 67-99; Romanian translation: 'Teologia Imnului Acatist', translated by Alexandru Prelipcean, *Ort*, NS, 5 (2013), 2, 84-113];

-, 'Die Kirche als Ort des Leben und der Rettung in Christus nach den Kontakien Romanos' des Meloden', in *Einheit und Katholizi-*

tät der Kirche: Forscher aus dem Osten und Westen Europas an den Quellen des gemeinsamen Glaubens, Pro Oriente-Studientagung 'L' Unité et la Catholicité de l' Église' – 'Einheit und Katholizität der Kirche', Theresia HAINTHALER et alii (eds.), Sibiu, 27.-30. Juni 2007, Tyrolia, Innsbruck-Wien 2009, 309-317;

-, 'Ῥωμανὸς ὁ Μελωδὸς καὶ ποίηση τῶν Χριστουγένων', *Πειραϊκὴ Ἐκκλησία*, vol. 22 (2012), 243, 10-13;

-, 'Ὁ σωτὴρ ἁπάντων ἀνθρώπων, μάλιστα δὲ πιστευόντων, ἀνακαλεῖ', *Πειραϊκὴ Ἐκκλησία*, vol. 23 (2013), 248, 29-31;

-, 'Γνώση ζοφορόφος καί γνώση ζωήφορος μέσα ἀπό τή δραματουργία τοῦ κακοῦ στό κοντάκιο τοῦ Ρωμανοῦ τοῦ Μελωδοῦ «Εἰς τήν σταύρωσιν»', in Ἰωάννης ΚΟΥΡΕΜΠΕΛΕΣ, *Δῶς' μου λόγο, Λόγε. Μελέτες λόγῳ Θεολογίας*, Ἐκδόσεις Κυριακίδη, Θεσσαλονίκη 2013, 83-95;

KÖDER, Johannes, 'Kontakion und Politischer Vers', *JÖB*, vol. 33 (1983), 45-56;

-, 'Antikebezüge bei Romanos dem Meloden?', *Wiener Humanistische Blätter*, vol. 43 (2001), 106-127;

-, 'Romanos Melodos über das Mönchtum', in *Porphyrogenita. Essays on the History and Literature of Byzantium and the Latin East in Honour of Julian Chrysostomides*, Charalambos DENDRINOS et alii (eds.), Ashgate, London 2001, 187-197;

-, 'Anmerkungen zu dem Romanos-Papyrus Vindob. G 26225', *JÖB*, vol. 53 (2003), 23-26;

-, 'Konjekturvorschläge zu Hymnen des Romanos Melodos', *JÖB*, vol. 54 (2004), 97-112;

-, 'Imperial Propaganda in the Kontakia of Romanos the Melode', *DOP*, vol. 62 (2008), 275-292;

KRUEGER, Derek, 'Writing and Redemption in the Hymns of Romanos the Melodist', *BMGS*, vol. 27 (2003), 1, 2-44;

-, 'Romanos the Melodist and the Christian Self in Early Byzantium', in *Proceedings of the 21st International Congress of Byzantine Studies, London, 2006*, Elizabeth JEFFREYS (ed.), vol. I, Plenary Papers, Aldershot, Ashgate, 2006, 247-266 (republished under the title: 'Romanos the Melodist and the Christian Self', in

Derek KRUEGER, *Liturgical Subjects. Christian Ritual, Biblical Narrative and the Formation of the Self in Byzantium*, University of Pennsylvania Press, Philadelphia 2014, 29-65);

-, 'Textuality and Redemption: The Hymns of Romanos the Melodist', in Derek KRUEGER, *Writing and Holiness. The Practice of Autorship in the Early Christian East*, series 'Divinations: Rereading Late Ancient Religion', University of Pennsylvania Press, Philadelphia 2011, 159-188;

-, 'The Internal Lives of Biblical Figures in the Hymns of Romanos the Melodist', în: *Adamantius. Rivista del Gruppo Italiano di Ricerca su 'Origine e la tradizione alessandrina'/ Journal of the Italian Research Group on 'Origen and the Alexandrian Tradition'*, vol. 19 (2013), 290-302;

KRYPIAKIEWICZ, P.F., 'De hymni acathisti auctore', *ByZ*, vol. 18 (1909), 2, 357-382;

KUEHN, Clement A., 'Dioskoros of Aphrodito and Romanos the Melodist', *BASPap*, vol. 27 (1990), 103-107;

Λ., Σωφρόνιος, 'Ῥωμανός ὁ Μελωδός καὶ ἡ Ἀκάθιστος', *GrēgPal*, vol. 1 (1917), 5, 193-207 (part I); 6, 269-280 (part II: *Ὁ χρόνος τῆς ἀκμῆς τοῦ Ῥωμανοῦ*); 13, 625-634 (part III: *Ῥωμανοῦ τοῦ Μελῳδοῦ: ἡ συγγενεία τῆς Ἀκαθίστου (1). Πρὸς τὰ ἔργα τοῦ Ῥωμανοῦ*); 14, 641-649 (part IV); 15, 817-819 (part VI);

LAMPSIDES, O., 'Über Romanos den Meloden. Ein unveröffentlicher hagiographischer Text', *ByZ*, vol. 61 (1968), 1, 36-39;

ΛΑΒΡΙΩΤΗ, Ἀλεξάνδρου, 'Περὶ Ῥωμανοῦ τοῦ Μελῳδοῦ', *EkklAl*, 11 (1892), 32, 255-256 (part I); 33, 262-264 (part II);

-, 'Ῥωμανοῦ τοῦ Μελῳδοῦ κοντάκιον εἰς τὰ ἅγια Φῶτα', *EkklAl*, 12 (1893), 48, 385-386 (part I); 50, 404 (part II);

LEVY, K., 'An Early Chant for Romanos' Contacium trium puerorum?', *CM*, vol. 22 (1961), 172-175;

LIEBER, Laura, 'Portraits of Righteousness: Noah in Early Christian and Jewish Hymnography', *ZRGG*, vol. 61 (2009), 4, 332-355 (about Romanos, 341-345);

LINGAS, Alexander, 'The Liturgical Place of the Kontakion in Constantinople', in *Liturgy, Architecture and Art in Byzantine*

World, Paper of the XVIII International Byzantine Congres (Moscow, 8-15 August 1991), Constantin C. AKENTIEV (ed.), col. 'Bizantinorossica', 1, St. Petersburg 1995, 50-57;
ΛΙΒΑΔΑΡΑΣ, Νικόλαος Α., 'Περὶ τὰ προβλήματα τῶν πατμιακῶν κοντακαρίων', *EEBS*, vol. 24 (1954), 337-347;
-, 'Üeber die Randnotizen der Kontakaria von Patmos (Codices 212=P und 213=Q)', *EEBS*, vol. 33 (1964), 17-47;
LOMBARDI-GIORDANO, C., 'Dans le contakion l'origine de l'«oratorio». Dans la musique byzantine l'origine de la polyphonie', *Actes du XIVe Congrès International d'Études Byzantines*, M. BERZA, E. STANESCU (eds.), vol. 3, Academia Republicii Socialiste România, București 1976, 531-536;
LOUTH, Andrew, 'Christian hymnography: from Romanos the Melodist to John Damascene', *Journal of Eastern Christian Studies*, vol. 57 (2005), 3-4, 195-206 (Romanian translation: 'Imnografia creștină de la Sf. Roman Melodul la Sfântul Ioan Damaschinul', in Sfântul ROMAN MELODUL, *Imnele Pocăinței* ..., 7-24);
MAAS, Paul, 'Die Chronologie der Hymnen des Romanos', *ByZ*, vol. 15 (1906), 1, 1-44;
-, 'Zu Romanos 18.ι', *ByZ*, vol. 16 (1907), 1, 257;
-, 'Grammatische und metrische Umarbeitungen in der Überlieferung des Romanos', *ByZ*, vol. 16 (1907), 2, 565-587;
-, 'Das Kontakion (Mit einem Exkurs über Romanos und Basileios von Seleukeia)', *ByZ*, vol. 19 (1910), 2, 285-306;
-, 'Kontakion auf den heiligen Theodoros unter dem Namen des Romanos', *OrChr*, 2 (1912), 48-63;
-, 'Ein Romanos-Zitat aus einer kappadozischen Inschrift?', *BNGJ*, vol. 3 (1922), 80;
-, 'Das Weihnachtslied des Romanos', *ByZ*, vol. 24 (1923-1924), 1, 1-13;
-, 'Romanos auf Papyrus', *Byz*, vol. 14 (1939), 1, 381;
MAISANO, Riccardo, 'L'accoglienza dei contaci di Romano il Melodo in Occidente', in *Politica, cultura e religione nell' impero romano (secoli IV-VI) tra Oriente e Occidente (Atti del Secondo*

Convengo dell' Associazione di Studii Tardoantiche), Fabrizio CONCA et alii (ed.), M. D'Auria Editore, Napoli 1993, 111-126;
-, 'Progetto di un lessico di Romano il Melode', in *Medioevo Romanzo e Orientale. Oralità, scrittura, modelli narrativi (Il Colloquio Internazionale Napoli, 17-19 febbraio 1994)*, Antonio PIOLETTI/Francesca RIZZO NERVO (eds.), Rubbettino, Soveria Mannelli 1995, 247-313;
-, 'Rispondenze formali tra proemio, strofe e ritornello nei Cantici di Romano il Melodo', *Studi sull'oriente cristiano*, vol. 6 (2002), 1, 77-100;
-, 'Funzione letteraria della citazioni bibliche nelle preghiere dei contaci di Romano il Melodo', in *Ad Contemplandam Sapientiam. Stuidi di Filologia, Letteratura Storia in memoria di Sandro Leanza*, Soveria MANNELLI (ed.), Rubbettino, Soveria Mannelli 2004, 369-378;
-, 'Le fonti patristiche di Romano il Melode', *Νέα Ῥώμη*, vol. 3 (2006), 89-114;
-, 'La croce nei contaci di Romano il Melodo', in *La Croce. Iconografia e interpretazione (secoli I – inizio XVI)*, Atti del Convegno internazionale di Studi (Napoli. 6-11 dicembre 1999), B. ULIANICH (ed.), vol. 3, Napoli 2007, 75-87;
-, 'Romanos's Use of Greek Patristic Sources', *DOP*, vol. 62 (2008), 261-274;
-, 'Spunti di esegesi biblica tra Romano il Melodo e Grigorio Magno', *Byzantina Mediterranea: Festschrift für Johannes Koder zum 65. Geburtstag*, Klaus BELKE et alii (eds.), Böhlau, Wien-Köln-Weimar 2007, 399-406;
ΜΑΡΤΖΕΛΟΥ, Γεωργίου, 'Ἡ χριστολογία τοῦ Βασιλείου Σελευκίας καὶ ὁ Ῥωμανὸς ὁ Μελῳδός', in *Χριστιανικὴ Θεσσαλονίκη* (Γ΄ Ἐπιστημονικό Συμπόσιο μὲ θέμα: Χριστιανικὴ Θεσσαλονίκη ἀπὸ τῆς Ἰουστινιάνειου ἐποχῆς ἕως καὶ τῆς Μακεδονικῆς δυναστείας), Ἐκδόσεις Δῆμος Θεσσαλονίκης (Κέντρου Ἱστορίας τοῦ δήμου Θεσσαλονίκης), Θεσσαλονίκη 1991, 97-166;
-, 'Die Mariologie des Basileios von Seleukeia und Romanos der Melode', in *Marienfrömmigkeit in Ost und West: Auf der Suche*

nach der Seele Europas: Marienfrömmigkeit in Ost und West. Studientagung der Pro Oriente-Sektion Salzburg aus Anlass ihres 20jährigen Bestehens, 7. und 8. Oktober 2005, Peter HOFRICHTER (ed.), Tyrolia, Innsbruck 2007, 43-66;

MERCATI, S.G., 'Note d'epigraphia bizantina. Il testo dell' inscrizione n. 65 di Inscriptions byzantines de la région d'Urgub en Cappadoce' e di Romano il Melode', *Bess.*, vol. 24 (1920), 199-201;

MIONI, Elpidio R., 'I kontakaria del Monte Athos', *AIVS*, 2/96, Veneţia, 1936-1937, 23-87;

-, 'Osservazioni sulla tradizione manoscritta di Romano il Melode', *Atti del V Congresso Internazionale di Studi Bizantini*, Roma 20-26 settembre 1936, vol. 1: Storia-Filologia-Diritto, *SBNE*, 5, Tipografia del Senato, Roma, 1939, 507-513;

MIRALLES, C., 'Los tres «Himnos a la Natividad» atribuidos a San Romano', *Boletin del Instituto de Estudios Helénicos*, vol. 2 (1968), 17-28;

MITSAKIS, Kariophilis, 'The Vocabulary of Romanos the Melodist', *Glotta*, vol. 43 (1965), 1-2, 171-197;

-, 'The Hymography of the Greek Church in the Early Christian Centuries', *JÖB*, vol. 20 (1971), 31-49;

MOROZOWICH, Mark M., '«Akathistos» and «kontakia»: structure, principles, guidelines', *EcOra*, vol. 22 (2005), 3, 361-374;

MOSKHOS, Mikhalis, 'Romanos' Hymn on the Sacrifice of Abraham: A Discussion of the Sources and a Translation', *Byz*, vol. 44 (1974), 2, 310-328;

MUREŞANU, Teodora, 'Apariţia, dezvoltarea şi afirmarea imnografiei bizantine până la Sfântul Roman Melodul', *Studia Universitatis Babes-Bolyai – Theologia Orthodoxa*, vol. 56 (2011), 1, 263-272;

NICKAU, Klaus, 'Justinian und der Nika-Aufstand bei Romanos dem Meloden: zum Kontakion 54 M.-Tr.', *ByZ*, vol. 95 (2003), 2, 603-620;

ΝΙΚΟΛΟΠΟΥΛΟΣ, Παναγ. Γ., "Ἐπὶ τὰς πηγὰς τοῦ εἰς τὴν θυσίαν τοῦ Ἀβραὰμ ὕμνου Ῥωμανοῦ τοῦ Μελῳδοῦ', *Athēna*, vol. 56 (1952), 278-285;

-, 'Ἐπὶ τῆς ἐπιγραφῆς καὶ τοῦ προοιμίου τοῦ εἰς τὸ Σάββατον τῆς Τυροφάγου ὕμνου Ῥωμανοῦ τοῦ Μελῳδοῦ', in *Πεπραγμένα του Θ' Διεθνούς Βυζαντινογικού Συνεδρίου*, vol. 3: Ἀνακοινώσεις: Ε' Λαογραφία, Στ' Φιλολογία Βυζαντινή, Ζ' Φιλολογία Μεταβυζαντινή, Ἀθήνα 1958, 184-187;

OLSEN, Nanna Liv, 'To byzantiniske hymner af Romanos Melodos [Om Guds Moder og Maria ved korset]', *Religion*, 4 (2004), 14-29;

PAPADOPOULOS-KERAMEUS, A., 'Mitteilungen über Romanos', *ByZ*, vol. 2 (1893), 3, 599-605;

-, 'Ὁ τῆς ἀκμῆς τοῦ Ῥωμανοῦ χρόνος', *Νέα Ἡμέρα*, 22-24 Ἰουλίου 1902, 1438;

> Review: PÉTRIDÈS, S., 'II. A. Papadopoulos-Kerameus: Ὁ τῆς ἀκμῆς τοῦ Ῥωμανοῦ χρόνος. Dans la Νέα ἡμέρα de Trieste, 22 et 24 juillet 1902', *EOr*, vol. 7 (1904), 44, 61.

-, 'Ῥωμανὸς καὶ Ἰωάννης Δαμασκηνός', *ByZ*, vol. 14 (1905), 1, 234-236;

-, 'Λείψανον κονδακαρίου σιναϊτικοῦ', *ByZ*, vol. 16 (1907), 1, 202-203;

ΠΑΠΑΓΙΑΝΝΗ, Γρηγορίου, 'Παρατηρήσεις στὸ Κοντάκιο τοῦ Ῥωμανοῦ τοῦ Μελῳδοῦ «Εἰς τὴν πόρνην»', in *Λόγια καὶ δημώδης γραμματεία τοῦ Ἑλληνικοῦ Μεσαίωνα. Πρακτικὰ Θ΄ Ἐπιστημονικῆς Συνάντησης (11-13 Μαΐου 2000). Ἀφιέρωμα στὸν Εὔδοξο Θ. Τσολάκη*, Ἐκδόσεις Ἀριστοτελίου Πανεπιστημίου Θεσσαλονίκης, Θεσσαλονίκη 2002, 85-109;

PAPOUTSAKIS, Manolis, 'The Making of a Syriac Fable: from Ephrem to Romanos', *Muséon*, vol. 120 (2007), 1-2, 29-75;

ΠΑΡΑΝΙΚΑΣ, Μαθαίος, 'Περὶ χριστιανικῆς ποιήσεως τῶν Ἑλλήνων', *Ἐπετηρὶς Φιλολογικοῦ Συλλόγου Κωνσταντινουπόλεως*, vol. 8 (1874), 174-194 (part I); 9 (1875), 119-130 (part II); 10 (1875), 10-22 (part III);

-, 'Περὶ Ῥωμανοῦ τοῦ Μελῳδοῦ', *EkklAl*, 12 (1982), 18, 141-143, 287-288;

-, 'Ρωμανοῦ τοῦ μελῳδοῦ Κοντάκια εἰς τὰ ἅγια φῶτα', *VV*, 5 (1898), 681-696;
PATON, Lucy Allen, 'A Note on the Vision of Romanos', *Spec.*, vol. 7 (1932), 4, 553-555;
PELTOMAA, Leena Mari, 'Herodias in the Poetry of Romanos the Melodist', *JÖB*, vol. 56 (2006), 77-99;
-, 'Female characters in the poetry of Romanos the Melodist', in *Proceedings of the 21st International Congress of Byzantine Studies: London, 21-26 August 2006*, vol. II: Abstracts of Panel Papers, Elizabeth JEFFREYS, Judith GILLILAND (eds.), Ashgate Publishing, Ashgate 2006, 37-38;
-, 'Romanos the Melodist and the Intercessory Role of Mary', in *Byzantina Mediterranea: Festschrift für Johannes Koder zum 65. Geburtstag*, Klaus BELKE et alii (eds.), Böhlau, Wien-Köln-Weimar 2007, 495-502;
-, 'Roles and Functions of Mary in the Hymnography of Romanos Melodos', *StPatr*, vol. 44 (2010), 487-498;
-, 'The Portrayal of the Wife of Potiphar by Romanos Melodos', in *ΔΩΡΟΝ ΡΟΔΟΠΟΙΚΙΛΟΝ: Studies in Honour of Jan Olof Rosenqvist*, Denis SEARBY et alii (eds.), *AUU.SByU*, 12, Uppsala Universitet, Uppsala 2012, 195-206;
-, '«*Cease your lamentations, I shall become an advocate for you*». Mary as Intercessor in Romanos' Hymnography', in *Presbeia Theotokou. The Intercessory Role of Mary across Times and Places in Byzantium (4th-9th Century)*, Leena Mari PELTOMAA et alii (eds.), Verlag der Österreichischen Akademie der Wissenschaften, Wien 2015, 131-137;
PELLEGRINO, M., '«Ἀσήπτων ξύλων» (Romano il Melode, Inno di Noè γ. 1)', *RSLR*, vol. 1 (1965), 108-109;
PETERSEN, William L., 'Romanos and the Diatessaron: Readings and Method', *NTS*, vol. 29 (1983), 484-507 [republished in: *Patristic and Text-Critical Studies: The Collected Essays of William L. Petersen*, Jan KRANS/Joseph VERHEYDEN (eds.), col. 'New Testament Tools. Studies and Documents', 40, Brill, Leiden 2012, 20-46];

-, 'The Dependence of Romanos the Melodist upon the Syriac Ephrem: Its Importance for the Origin of the Kontakion', *VigChr*, vol. 39 (1985), 2, 171-187 (republished in: *Patristic and Text-Critical Studies* ..., 47-61);

-, 'A New Testimonium to a Judaic-Christian Gospel Fragment from a Hymn of Romanos the Melodist', *VigChr*, vol. 50 (1996), 2, 105-116 (republished in: *Patristic and Text-Critical Studies* ..., 260-271);

-, 'The Dependence of Romanos *the Melodist* upon the Syriac Ephrem', *StPatr*, vol. 18-4 (1990), 274-281 (republished in: *Patristic and Text-Critical Studies*, 152-160);

PETRESCU, I.D., 'Cuviosul Roman cântărețul', *Predania*, 1 (1937), 3, 3-5 (republished in: *Predania și un Îndreptar ortodox cu, de și despre Nae Ionescu teolog*, antologie prefațată și realizată de Ioan I. Ică jr., Deisis, Sibiu 2001, 43-45);

PETRIDES, Sophrone, 'Office inédite de Saint Romain le Mélode', *ByZ*, vol. 11 (1902), 2, 358-369;

> Review: BARDOU, L., 'S. Pétridès: *Office inédit de saint Romain le Mélode*, Dans la *Byzantinische Zeitschrift*, t. XI, p. 358-369', *EOr*, vol. 6 (1903), 39, 159.

-, 'Saint Romain le Mélode', *EOr*, vol. 9 (1906), 59, 225-226;

ΠΕΖΟΠΟΥΛΟΥ, Ε., 'Περὶ τῆς μουσικῆς τοῦ Ῥωμανοῦ τοῦ Μελῳδοῦ', *Νέα Φόρμιγξ*, 1 (1921), 13-14;

PONS PONS, G., 'La infancia del Salvador en los himnos de Romano el Cantor: la misión de la Virgen María y de San José', *Estudios Josefinos*, 66 (2012), 205-236;

PORTER, Stanley E./PORTER, Wendy J., 'P. Vindob. G 26225: A New Romanos Melodus Papyrus in the Vienna Collection', *JÖB*, vol. 52 (2002), 135-148;

PREDA, Sabin/MARCHIȘ, Iustin, 'Sf. Roman Melodul – Condacul Întâmpinării Domnului', *AltBan*, NS, 11 (2000), 1-3, 123-154;

PREDA, Sabin, 'Condacul *Fecioara astăzi* ... alcătuit de Sf. Roman Melodul – analiza condacului pe baza structurii literare interne și a structurii melodice', *AFTOUB*, vol. 4 (2003-2004), 343-355;

-, [Studiu introductiv] on the Romanian translation: 'Sf. Roman Melodul, *Luna lui iulie în douăzeci de zile. Condac la pomenirea Sfântului Prooroc Ilie*', *StTeol*, SN, 4 (2008), 3, 143-147;

PRELIPCEAN, Alexandru, 'Sfântul Roman Melodul – imnograful desăvârșit al Ortodoxiei', *StTeol*, NS, 7 (2011), 2, 59-105;

-, 'De la imaginile neo-testamentare la imnografia secolului al VI-lea: Condacul *La nunta cea din Cana* (Εἰς τὸν ἐν Κανὰ γάμον) al Sf. Roman Melodul. Perspectiva istorică, aspectele filologice și teologia sa', in *Studia Theologica Doctoralia*, Viorel SAVA et alii (eds.), vol. 3, Doxologia, Iași 2011, 379-405;

-, 'Drama dialogală dintre omul cel vechi și Hristos – lumina cea neapropiată sau despre erminia hristologică a primului condac al Sfântului Roman Melodul închinat Epifaniei', *Ort*, NS, 4 (2012), 1, 106-122;

-, 'O nouă specie a imnografiei bizantine: condacul. Scurtă introducere în elementele sale definitorii', in *Sfântul Roman Melodul, Imnele Sfintei Scripturi ...*, Alexandru PRELIPCEAN/Alexandru IORGA (eds.), 13-79 [republished in *TV*, NS, 23 (2013), 1-4, 95-125];

-, '«From Adam to Moses»: the Typology of the Old Testament characters from the kontakia of Romanos the Melodist and its Assessment on the *Great Canon* of Andrew of Crete', *Review of Ecumenical Studies*, vol. 7 (2015), 3, 388-421 [Romanian translation: 'Tipologia Vechiului Testament în condacele lui Roman Melodul și Canonul cel Mare al lui Andrei Criteanul', in *Interpretarea biblică între Biserică și Universitate*, Alexandru IONIȚĂ (ed.), col. 'Studia Oecoumenica', 10, Andreiană, Presa Universitară Clujeană, Sibiu-Cluj-Napoca 2016, 260-302];

-, 'The Influence of Romanos the Melodist on the *Great Canon* of Saint Andrew of Crete: Some Remarks about Christological Typologies', *StPatr*, vol. 96 (2017), 441-450;

-, 'Condacul *la neofiți* al Sfântului Roman Melodul: de la poezie la argumentare istorică și viceversa', in *Cercetare și dialog teologic astăzi*, Viorel SAVA (ed.), col. 'Studia Theologica Doctoralia', 9, Doxologia, Iași 2017, 536-555;

-, 'The Eucharist and Its Interpretation in the Romanos of Melodist's Kontakia', in *Orientalia Patristica. Papers of the International Patristic Symposium*, May 1-4, 2017, Didahia Severin Publishing, Drobeta-Turnu-Severin, 2018, 290-299 (Romanian translation: 'Euharistia și interpretarea ei în condacele romaneice', in *Orientalia Patristica* ..., 594-603);

RÖMER, Cornelia Eva, 'Romanus Melodus auf einem Wiener Pergament', *ZPE*, vol. 109 (1995), 298-300;

RODGERS, Barbara Saylor, 'Romanos Melodos on the Raising of Lazarus', *ByZ*, vol. 107 (2014), 2, 811-830;

ROGOBETE, Cristina Costena, 'Cuviosul Roman Melodul – Imnele Epifaniei – traducere și comentariu', *AFTOUB*, vol. 2 (2001-2002), 493-522;

ROSSUM, Joost van, 'Romanos le Mélode et le Kontakion', *L'Hymnographie: Conférences Saint-Serge*, A.M. TRIACCA et A. PISTOIA (eds.), 46ᵉ Semaine d'Etudes Liturgiques (juin 1999), Edizioni Liturgiche, Roma, 2000, 93-104;

RUSU, Cristina, 'Poezia imnografică liturgică. Forme de dialogare juxtapuse și ambiguitatea în imnurile lui Roman Melodul și imnurile Sfântului Simeon Noul Teolog', *Poezia*, 13 (2008), 2, 208-213;

QUISPEL, Gilles, 'The Diatessaron of Romanos', in *New Testament Textual Criticism. Its Significance for Exegesis. Essays in Honour of B.M. Metzger*, Eldon Jay EPP and Gordon D. FEE (eds.), Clarendon Press, Oxford 1981, 305-311;

SALVANESCHI, Enrica, 'Adattamento interlinguistico come mezzo espressivo in Romano Melodo', *AMAT*, vol. 39 (1974), 21-68;

SCHORK, R.J., 'The Medical Motif in the Kontakia of Romanos the Melodist', *Tr.*, vol. 16 (1960), 353-363;

-, 'Typology of the *Kontakia* of Romanos', *StPatr*, vol. 6 (1962), 211-220;

-, 'The Sung Sermons', *Worship*, vol. 47 (1973), 9, 527-539;

-, 'Romanos, On Joseph I, stanza a: Text and Type', *Byz*, vol. 45 (1975), 1, 131-144;

-, 'Sung Sermons: Melodies, Morals and Biblical Interpretations in Byzantium', *BiRe*, vol. 7 (1991), 2, 20-27, 48;

SCHROEDER, Matthew, 'Romanus the Melodist: drama as an Instrument of Theology', *Logos*, vol. 43-45 (2002-2004), 203-251;

SICHEM, Paul Van, 'L'hymne sur Noé de Romanos le Mélode. Contribution à l'étude des sources', *EEBS*, 36 (1968), 27-36;

-, 'Een opstandingskontakion van Romanos de Melode als voorbeld van zijn dichtkunst', in *Ἀνάμνησις, Gedenkboek Prof. dr. E. A. Leemans*, R. THIBAU and H. DE LEY (eds.), 'De Tempel', Brügge 1970, 385-400;

STEVENSON, H., 'L'hymnographie de l'église grecque. Du rythme dans les cantiques de la liturgie grecque', *RQH*, vol. 20 (1876), 482-543;

STICHEL, Rainer, 'Naturwissenschaftliche Kenntnis des Romanos im Noe-Hymnus', *Hermes*, vol. 100 (1972), 2, 249-251;

SUTTNER, Ernst Chr., 'Die Ohnmacht der Mächtigen bei Romanos dem Meloden', *OS*, vol. 21 (1972), 1, 50-53;

SWART, G., 'The Cristus Patiens and Romanos the Melodist: Some Considerations on Dependence and Dating', *ACl*, vol. 33 (1990), 53-64;

ŠIRCA, Alien, 'Ekfrazno posništvo pri Romanu Melodu in Pavlu Silentiariju', *Ars et Humanitas*, vol. 11 (2017), 1, 63-74;

TARAGNA, Anna Maria, 'Il sorriso di Gesù. Una nota sui contaci di Romano il Melodo', in *Riso e comicità nel cristianesimo antico*, Atti del Convegno di Torino, 14-16 febbraio 2005, e altri studi, Clementina MAZZUCCO (ed.), Edizioni dell' Orso, Alessandria 2007, 779-791;

TIERNEY, J.J., 'Romano il Melode: la vita e l'opera', *IKBS*, vol. 7 (1953), 208-213;

ΤΩΜΑΔΑΚΗΣ, Νικόλαος Β., 'Ἡ ἐκκλησιαστικὴ ἡμῶν ποίησις καὶ ἡ συμφωνία αὐτῆς πρὸς τὸ δόγμα καὶ πρὸς τὰ κείμενα τῶν Γραφῶν', *Athēna*, vol. 53 (1949), 94-118;

-, 'Ῥωμανοῦ Μελῳδοῦ κοντάκιον εἰς τὸν ὅσιον πατέρα ἡμῶν Νικόλαον κατὰ τὸν πατμιακὸν κώδικα 212 ἐκδιδόμενον', *Athēna*, vol. 55 (1951), 155-188, 225;

-, 'Pourquoi nous sommes passés du Kontakion au canon', *RSBN*, vol. 7 (1953), 214;
-, 'Ῥωμανὸς καὶ ἅγιος Δημήτριος. Ἁγιολογικαὶ καὶ ὑμνογραφικαὶ ἐπιστασίαι', *Athēna*, vol. 59 (1955), 86-130;

> *Review*: GUILLAND, R., '*Tomadakis (N. B.)* Ῥωμανὸς καὶ Ἅγιος Δημήτριος. Ἁγιολογικαὶ καὶ ὑμνολογικαὶ ἐπιστασίαι. *Romanos le mélode et saint Démétrius. Réponse au R.P.P. Ioannou; avec un sommaire en française.* Athènes. 1955, 51 p.', *REG*, vol. 69 (1956), 324, 263.

-, 'Ῥωμανικά Μελετήματα: Α'. Ὁ ἐσωτερικὸς διάλογος τῶν ὕμνων τοῦ Ῥωμανοῦ τοῦ Μελῳδοῦ. Β'. Ἀνεκδότος ὕμνος Ῥωμανοῦ τοῦ Μελῳδοῦ εἰς τὸν πατριάρχη Κωνσταντινοπώλεος Ἰωάννην τὸν Χρυσόστομον. Γ'. Ἡ πατερική γνῶσις Ῥωμανοῦ τοῦ Μελῳδοῦ', *EEBS*, vol. 26 (1956), 3-36;
-, 'Αἰσθητικὴ διαφοροποίησις θρησκευτικῆς καὶ ἐκκλησιαστικῆς ὑμνογραφίας', *EEBS*, vol. 28 (1958), 65-89;
-, 'Ἡ γέννησις τοῦ Χριστοῦ ὑμνούμενη ἀπό τόν Ῥωμανόν Μελῳδόν', *Λογοτεχνικά Χρονικά*, vol. 2 (1970), 145-150;
-, 'Ὁ Ῥωμανός ὁ Μελῳδός δέν εἶναι ὁ συγγραφέας τοῦ Ἀκαθίστου', *Athēna*, vol. 72 (1971), 3-24 (Italian translation: 'Romano il Melode non è l'autore dell'Inno Acatisto', in *Studii Filologici e Storici in Onore di V. de Falco. Études de philology et d'histoire*, Libreria Scientifica Editrice, Napoli 1971, 497-519);
-, 'Romanus Melodus and the Greek Tragedians', in *Serta Turyniana. Studies in Greek Literature and Palaeography in honor of Alexander Turyn*, John L. HELLER and J.K. NEWMAN (eds.), University of Illionois Press, Urbana 1974, 401-409;
TOPPING, Eva Catafygiotu, 'Romanos: Ikon of a Poet', *GOTR*, vol. 12 (1966), 92-111;
-, 'A Byzantine Song for Symeon: The Fourth Kontakion of St. Romanos', *Tr.*, vol. 24 (1968), 409-420;
-, 'The Poet-Priest in Byzantium', *GOTR*, vol. 14 (1969), 31-41;
-, 'The Apostle Peter, Justinian and Romanos the Melodos', *BMGS*, vol. 2 (1976), 1-15;

-, 'St. Romanos the Melodist and his First Nativity Kontakion', *GOTR*, vol. 21 (1976), 231-250;
-, 'Romanos, On the Entry into Jerusalem: «a Basilikos Logos»', *Byz*, vol. 47 (1977), 65-91;
-, 'Mary at the Cross: St. Romanos' Kontakion for Holy Friday', *ByS(P)*, vol. 4 (1977), 18-37;
-, 'On Earthquakes and Fires: Romanos' Encomium to Justinian', *ByZ*, vol. 71 (1978), 1, 22-35;
-, 'St. Romanos the Melodos: Prince of Byzantine Poets', *GOTR*, vol. 24 (1979), 1, 65-75;
-, 'Ὁ Ἅγ. Ρωμανὸς ὁ Μελῳδὸς καὶ ὁ πρῶτος ὕμνος του εἰς τὴν γέννησιν', in *Three Byzantine Sacred Poets. Studies of Saint Romanos Melodos, St. John of Damascus and St. Symeon the New Theologian*, N.M. VAPORIS (ed.), Brookline/Mass. 1979, 12-34;
-, 'Romanos on Judas: A Byzantine Ethopoeia', *Byzantiaka*, vol. 2 (1982), 9-27;
TRIGG, Joseph Wilson, 'Romanos's biblical interpretation: drama, imagery, and attention to the text', in *In Dominico Eloquio - In Lordly Eloquence: esssay on Patristic exegesis in honor of Robert Louis Wilken*, Paul M. BLOWERS et alii (eds.), William B. Eerdmans Publishing Company, Grand Rapids, Michigan-Cambridge 2002, 380-394;
TOSI, Renzo, 'Il ladro derzbato in Romano il Melode (23, 14 M.-T.)', *Νέα Ῥώμη*, vol. 1 (2004), 59-64;
TRYPANIS, C.A., 'Romanos the Melodist', in *The Orthodox Ethos. Essays in honor of the Centenary of the Greek Orthodox Archdiocese of North and South America*, A.J. PHILIPPOU (ed.), Holywell Press, Oxford 1964, 186-199;
-, 'An Anonymous Early Byzantine Kontakion on the Virgin Mary', *ByZ*, vol. 58 (1965), 2, 327-332;
-, 'The Metres of Romanos', *Byz*, vol. 36 (1966), 1, 560-623;
-, 'Οὗτος and αὐτός in Romanos', *ByZ*, vol. 64 (1971), 1, 33-34;
-, 'The Date of the Early Byzantine Kontakion on the Holy Fathers of Nicaea', *ByZ*, vol. 61 (1968), 1, 19-26;

-, 'Romanos Melodos', *Byzantine Studies in Australia: Newsletter*, 6 (1980), 8;

TUILIER, André (ed.), '*Le* Christus patiens *et Romanos le Mélode*', in *Grégoire de Nazianze. La passion du Christ. Tragédie*, Introduction, texte critique, traduction, notes et index de ..., col. 'Sources Chrétiennes', 149, Les Éditions du Cerf, Paris 1969, 39-47;

USPENSKIJ, N.D., 'Кондаки св. Романа Сладкопевца', *Богословские труды*, 4 (1968), 191-201;

> *Review*: P., V. I., 'N.D. Uspenski, *Condacele Sfântului Roman dulce cântătorul* publicat în *Studii Teologice*, Editura Patriarhiei din Moscova, vol. IV, 1968, pp. 191-201', *StTeol*, 23 (1971), 7-8, 589-590.

-, 'Романа Сладкопевец и его кондаки', *Журнал Московской Патриархии*, 11 (1966), 63-68 (part I); 12 (1967), 69-79 (part II);

VAILHE, S., 'Saint Romain le Mélode', *EOr*, vol. 5 (1902), 4, 207-212;

VAN DE VEN, P., 'Encore Romanos le mélode', *ByZ*, vol. 12 (1903), 1, 153-166;

> *Review*: PETRIDES, S., 'III. P. Van den Ven: *Encore Romanos le Mélode*. Dans *Byzantinische Zeitschrift*, t. XII (1903), p. 153-166', *EOr*, vol. 7 (1904), 44, 61.

VAN OMMESLAEGHE, Florent, 'Le dernier mot sur Romanos le Mélode', *AnBoll*, vol. 97 (1979), 3-4, 417-421;

-, 'La source de l'hymne sur s. Jean Chrysostome attribuée à Romain le Mélode', *AnBoll*, vol. 98 (1980), 3-4, 387-398;

VAN ROMPAY, Lucas, 'Romanos le Mélode: un poète syrien à Constantinople', in *Early Christian Poetry: A Collection of Essays*, J. DEN BOEFT, A. HILHORST (eds.), Brill, Leiden 1993, 283-296;

VASILEIEV, A., 'Время жизни Романа Сладкопѣвца', *VV*, 8 (1901), 435-478;

> *Review*: PETRIDES, S., 'I. Vasiliev: *La chronologie de Romain le Mélode* (en russe). Dans *Visantiiskii Vremennik*, t. VIII (1901), p. 435-478', *EOr*, vol. 7 (1904), 44, 61.

VASILIEVSKIJ, V.G., 'Когда жил Роман Сладкопевец?', *VV*, 1 (1894), 256-258;

VARVA, Gavril, 'Sfântul Roman Melodul: repere bio-bibliografice', *Renașterea*, 17 (2006), 10 (198), 12;

VOICESCU, Mihail, 'Nașterea Domnului în creația imnografică a Sfântului Roman Melodul', *StTeol*, 35 (1983), 1-2, 18-27;

-, 'Învierea Domnului în creația imnografică a Sfântului Roman Melodul', *GBis*, 42 (1983), 4-5, 239-250;

VOGT, Ernst, 'Das Akrostichon in der griechischen Literatur', *AuA*, vol. 13 (1967), 80-95;

WELLESZ, E., 'Kontakion and Kanon', *ICMS*, Roma, 1952, 131-133;

WIGGERMANN, Karl-Friedrich, '*Die Athener werden von den Galiläern besiegt*. Ein homiletisch-spiritueller Hymnus des Romanos Melodos', *JLH*, vol. 46 (2007), 160-169;

WINDELL, J., 'Imagery of the Cross. The Song of Praise to the Cross in Romanos: «The Adoration of the Cross»', *EkklPh*, vol. 66-67 (1984-1985), 54-62;

ZANNINI, Paolo M., 'Romano il Melode e le tematiche patristiche greco-siriache su Gv 2, 1-11', *Theotokos. Ricerche interdisciplinary di Mariologia*, 7 (1999), 1, 41-65;

-, 'Romano il Melode e le origini della mistagogia mariana a Bisanzio', *Mar.*, vol. 71 (2009), 175-176, 361-419;

ZUNTS, Günther, 'Probleme des Romanos-Textes', *Byz*, vol. 34 (1964), 2, 469-534;

-, 'The Romanos Papyrus', *JThS*, NS, vol. 16 (1965), 2, 463-468.

8. Notes

[ANONYMUS], 'Summaries of Dissertations for the Degree of Ph.D., 1929-30', *HSCP*, vol. 41 (1930), 191-192 ('Marjorie Carpenter, The Origin and the Influence of the Christmas Kontakion of Romanos');

DAGRON, Gilbert/THUILLIER, Jean Irigoin/ROBERT, Louis, 'Actes de l'Association: communications présentées en 1983-1984', *REG*, vol. 97 (1984), 462-464, xix ('*Communications*: M.P.L. Gatier, *Un élément de datations de l'oeuvre de Romanos le Mélode: à propos du premier hymne des dix Vierges*').

Studien zur Orientalischen Kirchengeschichte
hrsg. von Martin Tamcke

Claudia Rammelt (Hg.) in Verbindung mit Jan Gehm und Rebekka Scheler
Pluralität und Koexistenz, Gewalt, Flucht und Vertreibung
Christliche, jesidische und muslimische Lebenswelten in den gegenwärtigen Umbrüchen im Nahen Osten
Bd. 59, 2019, ca. 256 S., ca. 29,90 €, br., ISBN 978-3-643-14293-1

Kai Merten
Annahme und Ablehnung
Menschen mit Behinderungen in Kirche und Gesellschaft in Äthiopien
Bd. 58, , 136 S., 29,90 €, br., ISBN 978-3-643-14242-9

Symeon Tsolakidis (Hg.)
Die Chronik von Morea
Übersetzt, eingeleitet und mit Anmerkungen versehen von Symeon Tsolakidis
Bd. 57, , 344 S., 34,90 €, br., ISBN 978-3-643-14057-9

Christine Chaillot
Die Rolle der Bilder und die Ikonenverehrung in den Orientalischen Orthodoxen Kirchen
Syrische, Armenische, Koptische und Äthiopische Traditionen. Geleitworte von Prof. Dr. Martin Tamcke und Metropolit Damaskinos der Schweiz
Bd. 56, 2018, 144 S., 14,90 €, br., ISBN 978-3-643-90993-0

Christine Chaillot
The Role of Images and the Veneration of Icons in the Oriental Orthodox Churches
Syrian Orthodox, Armenian, Coptic, Ethiopian Traditions. Forewords by Dr Sebastian Brock and Metropolitan Damaskinos of Switzerland
vol. 55, 2018, 144 pp., 14,90 €, pb., ISBN 978-3-643-90985-5

Christine Chaillot
Rôle des images et vénération des icônes dans les Églises orthodoxes orientales
Traditions syriaque, arménienne, copte et éthiopienne
vol. 54, 2017, 124 pp., 14,90 €, br., ISBN 978-3-643-90958-9

Martin Tamcke (Hg.)
Partnerschaft, Freundschaft, Dialog
Beiträge zum internationalen Symposium am Lehrstuhl für Ökumenische Theologie und Orientalische Kirchen- und Missionsgeschichte der Georg-August-Universität Göttingen vom 20. bis 22. Juni 2015
Bd. 53, 2016, 190 S., 29,90 €, br., ISBN 978-3-643-13427-1

Svante Lundgren
Die Assyrer
Von Ninive bis Gütersloh
Bd. 52, 2016, 176 S., 19,90 €, br., ISBN 978-3-643-13256-7

Diradur Sardaryan
Surb Patarag – Die Heilige Liturgie der Armenischen Apostolischen Kirche
Eine Einführung
Bd. 51, 2017, 100 S., 19,90 €, br., ISBN 978-3-643-13154-6

LIT Verlag Berlin – Münster – Wien – Zürich – London
Auslieferung Deutschland / Österreich / Schweiz: siehe Impressumsseite

Andreas Müller (Hg.)
Das Kreuz unter dem Halbmond
Orientalische Christen im Angesicht des „Arabischen Frühlings"
Bd. 50, 2014, 168 S., 19,90 €, br., ISBN 978-3-643-12753-2

Martin Tamcke; Gladson Jathanna (Eds.)
Body, Emotion and Mind 'Embodying'
The Experiences in Indo-European Encounters
vol. 49, 2013, 264 pp., 34,90 €, br., ISBN 978-3-643-90426-3

Roland Werner
Das Christentum in Nubien
Geschichte und Gestalt einer afrikanischen Kirche
Bd. 48, 2013, 520 S., 59,90 €, br., ISBN 978-3-643-12196-7

Zeki Joseph
Das Buch der ergötzlichen Erzählungen des Bar Hebräus
Mit einem Vorwort von Martin Tamcke
Bd. 47, 2013, 128 S., 19,90 €, br., ISBN 978-3-643-11977-3

Najib George Awad
And Freedom Became a Public-Square
Political, Sociological and Religious Overviews on the Arab Christians and the Arabic Spring
vol. 46, 2012, 280 pp., 29,90 €, br., ISBN 978-3-643-90266-5

Martin Tamcke; Gladson Jathanna (Eds.)
Construction of the Other, Identification of the Self
German Mission in India
vol. 45, 2012, 400 pp., 69,90 €, pb., ISBN 978-3-643-90260-3

Kai Merten
Das äthiopisch-orthodoxe Christentum
Ein Versuch zu verstehen
Bd. 44, 2012, 352 S., 24,90 €, br., ISBN 978-3-643-11645-1

Hacik Rafi Gazer
Studien zum kirchlichen Schulwesen der Armenier im Kaukasus
Teil I: 19. Jahrhundert
Bd. 43, 2012, 144 S., 19,90 €, br., ISBN 978-3-643-11532-4

Paulos Mar Gregorios (Metropolit von Delhi)
Gebetbuch für junge Menschen
Gebete aus der indischen syrisch-orthodoxen Tradition. Herausgegeben von Martin Tamcke
Bd. 42, 2011, 72 S., 19,90 €, br., ISBN 978-3-643-11431-0

Magdi Rashidi Beshai Awad
Untersuchungen zur koptischen Psalmodie
Christologische und liturgische Aspekte
Bd. 41, 2007, 304 S., 34,90 €, br., ISBN 978-3-8258-0164-9

Martin Tamcke (Hg.)
„Dich, Ararat, vergesse ich nie!"
Neue Beiträge zum Schicksal Armeniens und der Armenier
Bd. 40, 2006, 136 S., 19,90 €, br., ISBN 3-2858-0018-0

LIT Verlag Berlin – Münster – Wien – Zürich – London
Auslieferung Deutschland / Österreich / Schweiz: siehe Impressumsseite